Pretty Me

A Handbook
For Being Your Best

Pretty Me

A Handbook
For Being Your Best

Linda G. Wilder Dyer

Illustrations by
Renatta Cochran Holt

Clairebrooke Press

For information, write:

Clairebrooke Press.
2129 General Booth Blvd., Suite 103-300
Virginia Beach, VA 23454

Use of this work as course or seminar text is prohibited
without the expressed written consent of the author.
Courses and seminars are available for girls ages 6 to 11
and 12 to 17 based on *Pretty Me: A Handbook For Being
Your Best,* and *Finishing Touches For Teens.*

Please address ordering inquiries to:

Hampton Roads Publishing Company
891 Norfolk Square
Norfolk, Virginia 23502
(804) 459-2453
FAX: (804)455-8907
Call toll-free 1-800-766-8009 (orders only).

Edited by Patricia Trainor-LeRoi
Cover design by Patrick Smith
Book design by Patrick Smith and Sherri Faye Caldow

Library of Congress Cataloging-in-Publication Data:

Dyer, Linda G. Wilder, 1954-

Pretty me: a handbook for being your best
by Linda G. Wilder Dyer; edited by Patricia Trainor-LeRoi
p.   cm.
Summary: A handbook for girls to help them form good habits
and feel good about what they say, the way they look, and how
they act.
ISBN 1-898901-13-3
1. Etiquette for girls [1. Etiquette 2. Beauty, Personal 3. Health
4. Conduct of life.] I. Trainor-LeRoi, Patricia II. Title
BJ1857.G5D94   1989   88-39076
395′.1233—dc 19   CIP
                                                   AC

ISBN 1-878901-13-3   10 9 8 7 6 5 4 3 2
Printed in the United States of America

For Ashley Brooke—my precious daughter and my husband, Courtney.

This book is dedicated to the memory of my parents Oscar and Hazel Wilder who always encouraged me to be the very best at whatever I pursued. They always believed in me, and I think they'd be very proud.

To Pat Hoke, I also dedicate this book, for she, too, has been my driving force and my inspiration to accomplish my goals.

A portion of the proceeds of this book will benefit The Easter Seal Society of Virginia, Inc.

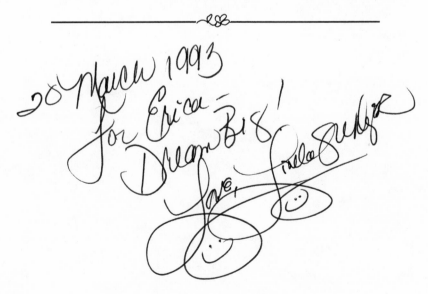

Contents

Acknowledgments

A project that has taken the better part of two years to complete has had ample time to accumulate folks who need to be recognized!

I'll try to be as brief as possible, but when you've just completed your first book, you are tempted (and feel somewhat obligated) to acknowledge and thank everyone from your second grade teacher to the man who sells you floppy discs.

Certainly, without the help of Karen Horner, my manuscript would have never reached the hands of my publisher on time. Her nimble fingers and keen mind made the words on my legal pads a tangible product.

My illustrator, friend, and associate, Renatta Holt, practically read my mind (as friends are often expected to do) to create wonderful memories in picture form.

Eugenia Seltzer and Anne Riggin of Miller & Rhoads in Richmond, Virginia; Betty Graham of Leggett in Norfolk, Virginia; and author-lecturer Catherine Lake have opened doors for me, which without their help may have been bolted shut.

On June 17, 1988, I walked into the president's office of Donning Publishers in Norfolk, Virginia and proceeded to do nothing short of tap dancing and singing "On the Good Ship Lollipop." I arrived armed with less than twenty pages of manuscript, a persuasive nature and every Dale Carnegie Course skill I ever learned! Quite frankly, I can't remember when I've prayed so hard! Thankfully, publisher Bob Friedman was receptive and open to giving the "new kid" a break, and turning her dream into a reality.

Barbara Lewis, owner of the longtime southern "landmark" of finishing schools, Charm Associates, has been instrumental in helping a chubby teenager's life-long goal of modeling turn into a home-town success story. It was that success and self-confidence that gave me the ability to teach young girls what I had been taught and to nurture the dream of this book into a reality.

Another reality that deserves acknowledgment is the fact that my family, friends, and co-workers have graciously dealt with being neglected and cut short in recent months. I knew there would be a light at the end of the tunnel. Thanks to all of you, it is beautiful and bright.

Introduction

Like a lot of grown-ups, I had a special person to help me feel better about myself while I was a young girl. What a helpful thing it is to have someone to go to when we have a question or a problem or just to listen to us when we want to talk about something.

My special person was my Aunt Liz. Her whole name was Mary Elizabeth Hackney. She was my mom's younger sister, and when I was growing up, she was like having the most wonderful big sister in the whole world! She understood everything about me. Now, I didn't say she went along with everything I wanted to do. (After all, she wouldn't let me sneak on the bus when she went home from visiting us one summer!)

Whenever my Mom would veto a special request, it was Aunt Liz whose shoulder I would cry on. After many tearful pleas in the fifth grade to have my ears pierced, it was none other than—you guessed it—my Aunt Liz who came to my rescue, and convinced my mom and dad that piercing my ears would not "brand me" for life. But it was also my Aunt Liz who taught me the value of taking good care of my skin, my hair, my clothes—and yes—the value of respecting my parents' wishes.

I wrote this book for many reasons, but the main reason is to help you always feel good about the things that you do and say, and about the way you look and act. No matter where you go or who you are with, I want you to be at ease. I will help you know what to do and what to say to make growing up a little easier. The years from now until you become a teenager should be exciting and happy times, times full of questions and answers, discovery and exploring.

This book will also help you to form all of the good habits that you'll need so that you'll always look your prettiest. Forming good habits when you're still young will make growing up as the "prettiest you" possible so much easier.

I wish I could meet each and every young girl who reads *Pretty Me*, but since that's impossible, I want this book to be your special friend. This *Pretty Me* book will be just like a best friend you can turn to for answers to your many questions about being the very best "you" that you can be.

It is my sincere wish that growing up be the happiest of times for you.

Virginia Beach, VA 1988   Linda G. Wilder Dyer

Treasures
All About *Pretty Me*

My name is *Erica John Newberry*

I live at 3100 Mollifield Lane

in Charlottesville, VA

City   State

My parents are *Yvonne* and *Linda*

My phone number is (804)973-0264

I have a pretty bedroom. I always try to keep it neat and clean so that I will be proud of it. (Especially when I have a sleep-over!) Here's a picture of my room (*or* ask Mother if you may cut out a picture of a magazine or catalog that looks like a room you'd love to have).

*Put a picture
of your room here*

Here's a picture of me when I first received my *Pretty Me* book.

Put *your*
picture here

My favorite color is are ___Pink, Blue, and Purple___

My favorite food is ___Pizza___

My favorite music is ___Sister act soundtrack___

My special friends are
1. Lori
2. Karah
3. Cory
4. Leslie
5. Elizibeth
6. Ellie
7. Alyson

15

EXERCISE DAILY

EAT WELL

SCIENCE

$$\begin{array}{r} 2 \\ 2 \\ + \\ \hline 4 \end{array}$$

MATH

I like to stay healthy by _exercise_
eat well

My favorite school
subjects are   _Math_
Science
Reading
History

(Because I know that a smart "me" is a pretty "me!")

The nicest thing about me is   My Smile

Chapter I
I Like Me

Getting along with all the people you will meet in your life is so important. Being pleasant to your parents, your brothers and sisters, your friends, your teachers, and all of the new people you will meet is a very important part of growing up.

Let's begin with the people you'll probably be with the most—your family. The relationship you will have with your parents is a very special one. There will be ups and downs, of course, just like with any relationship, but your mom and dad are the two main people in the entire world who care about you the most. While you may feel more comfortable telling your problems to a good friend instead of a parent, it is important to trust them—just as you will want them to trust you.

When I was only five years old, I learned one of my many lessons in trust from my mother. We were visiting one of her friends in our neighborhood while my dad was at work. While my mom and her friend were doing "mommy" things in the kitchen—drinking tea and trading recipes—I was allowed to sit in the living room and read. Now, that may not sound very exciting to you, but to me it was a treat that rated right up there with malted milk balls! The neighbor's living room was like a world of make believe. Figurines of every description stood like miniature princesses, lace hung from every window, and there seemed to be roses absolutely everywhere. I love to explore new places, don't you? Well, I explored a little too much I'm afraid, and a pink and white "princess" with pale yellow ringlets took a tumble! My mother and her friend were outside by now discussing those wonderful rose bushes so I knew that no one had heard the disaster. I felt very sick in my tummy, very quickly. I was always a typical girl, and even when I had my play clothes on, I carried my pocketbook everywhere. I quickly tucked the broken pieces in my purse and took a deep breath.

As my mom and I walked home I burst into tears, telling her everything. We went back to the neighbor's house, and she was so kind and understanding. She explained to me that because I was honest and came to my mom with the truth that she would always trust me. What I had done by telling her what happened was to show her that I trusted how she would react. Trust. It is such an important word. When you know that somebody really loves you, you will not be afraid to tell them everything that is on your mind.

Parents are considered your "elders." So are your grand-parents, great-grandparents, aunts, and uncles. Elders should always be treated with respect and trust. "Yes Ma'am," "No Ma'am," "Yes Sir," and "No Sir," are not old-fashioned and should be used routinely.

Here are a few helpful reminders:

Don't lie to your parents
Don't be late coming home (call if you are running late)
Don't exaggerate
Don't eavesdrop (on your parents or *anyone!*)
Don't forget "Please" and "Thank you," "Sir" and "Ma'am"

Your father probably works outside of your home. He may be tired and hungry when he gets home from work. My dad used to tell me that having me greet him cheerfully at the door when he got home made him forget how tired he was!

He might have been exaggerating just a little—but I didn't mind. It made me feel great. Remember that. Even if you have had a bad day at school, try not to unload all the problems of the entire day on your dad when he gets home. This is probably not a time to tell him you put his aftershave in your bubble bath!

The same advice goes for moms. Many more moms

work other jobs in addition to the *big* jobs they have at home. When I was a little girl, most of our moms did not work away from home. Mom had her hands full just getting everyone out of the house on time in the morning for school and work, keeping the house clean, doing the laundry, and probably making sure everyone got to ballet or soccer or both!

Well, moms still do that, but they may also work in an office, a hospital, a courtroom, a department store, a school—well, almost anywhere!

Later in your book we will talk about how to be more helpful around the house. This will be very helpful, especially if both your parents have outside jobs.

Being helpful and cheerful is probably something you do most of the time anyway, but it never hurts to have some gentle reminders.

Siblings. That's a strange sounding word, isn't it? Actually, it's just a fancy word that means brothers and sisters. No, no! Don't close this book here and now, threatening to hit your little brother over the head with it.

Seriously though, if you are going to live in the same house with different human beings, you are going to have differences every now and then. It is normal. It is expected. It is *not* the end of the world if your sister borrows your sweater or your teenage brother spends an hour in the bathroom!

It is a special (and memorable) part of growing up. You may have a hard time believing that now, but honestly, there will be a time when you will look back on some of the crazy antics of your brothers and sisters and not trade the experiences for anything!

Speaking of bathroom sharing, I know some families who like to use a schedule, sort of a sign-up sheet, and have it posted inside the medicine cabinet door telling who needs use of the bathroom and when. If you share a bathroom with a big brother or sister who has started dating, consider this mandatory!

If you have a sister, you may find that in addition to sharing a bathroom you will also be sharing a bedroom. It takes a lot of understanding and communication to be able to share something as personal as your living space. It is no doubt that you will need to establish some guidelines. It is a lot smarter to have a few ground rules to live by than to have unnecessary arguments later. If you and your sister are lucky enough to be the same size, then you've got it made! The two of you will have the advantage of having what will seem like two whole wardrobes! There's one very important thing that you will need to master though—closet organization. We will work on that in another chapter in your book.

Many of the same rules for getting along with your friends will be the rules you will want to apply to the friendship with your siblings.

Don't be bossy; be helpful.
Don't be boastful; be proud.
Don't be selfish; always share.
Don't criticize; find the good points.
Don't hold a grudge; accept apologies graciously.
Don't be a tattletale; be understanding.
Don't whisper; speak clearly and openly
around others.

If you will remember to give your brothers and sisters the same courtesy and consideration that you would give to your very best friends, you will be the lucky one.

When I was a little girl, I was so envious of my friends who had brothers and sisters. I had none. I used to cry and feel sorry for myself a lot. You can just imagine what sort of reaction I got from my friends with siblings! They thought I had lost my mind! Well, I want you to know that those same friends have very special friendships with their brothers and sisters today. To have a special friend who actually lived in your house with you seemed like a most special treat. I looked forward to the weekends most so I could ask a special friend to spend the night at my house. To me that was almost as good as having my own sister!

You will also want to get along well with:

Teachers or anyone who is an instructor. Always be willing to listen and learn. Pay attention in class. Don't interrupt or be giggly. Be thankful for the help and knowledge that your teachers share. Let them know how much you appreciate them. I'll bet it has been a long time since you walked up to one of your teachers and told him or her how much you appreciate them. The next time you want to leave school with a good feeling, just go up to your teacher and say, "Gee, that really was a neat class today!"

Waiters and Waitresses. Always use "Please" and "Thank You" when you order or ask for service. Don't treat these people like they are your personal "servants." Have respect for them and appreciate what they do for you.

Doctors, Dentists, and Nurses. Try not to be frightened or intimidated by them. Understand that these are special people who have had years of training just so that they could learn how to take care of people. Be a patient "Patient!" Don't become angry with them when they are trying to help you. Be as brave and courteous as possible.

Policemen, Firemen, and Paramedics. There are few jobs that have as much responsibility as these. When these people are busy doing their jobs, you mustn't interrupt. They must be able to concentrate very closely on what they are doing. If you happen to come upon the scene of an acci-dent, and there are already people there working, please stay out of the way. It is very tempting to stay and stare at what's going on but that can be very dangerous, not only to the people involved, but to you as well. You will enjoy oppor-tunities when policemen, firemen, or other community workers come to your schools to talk about what they do—perhaps at a Career Day. That's the time to be curious.

New Friends. I'm sure you have heard that you "should never judge a book by its cover." No truer words have ever been spoken. Don't base a friendship on where a person lives, or what clothes they wear, how much money their parents make, or what kind of car their parents drive. If you have always wanted an opportunity to act more grown up, here is your chance. It doesn't matter if they go to a different church or have a different color skin or speak differently than you. It also should not matter if they have a wheelchair or other equipment to aid them in doing the things they want to do. New friends come in all different shapes, sizes, colors and nationalities. Enjoy the variety!

Introductions

One of the nicest benefits of all the new self-confidence that you are gaining are the new friends you will meet. Some of them will be introduced to you by others; some you will go up to all by yourself and proudly announce, "Hi! I'm Sarah, the new girl in your math class. Do you walk home from school?" See, it's not so hard; actually, it's a lot of fun once you get the hang of it.

There's no doubt that you will want all of these new friends to meet each other as well. Then, of course, you will want them to visit your home and meet your family. Oh, am I making it sound complicated? It doesn't have to be if you follow a couple of simple rules: ladies first, elders first.

Well, maybe it's not quite that simple, but it doesn't have to frighten you to the point that you don't learn how to "share" all these new friends. That's right—share. Introducing someone you like to another person is just like sharing them! I don't know of a nicer gift to give—or to receive. Let's discuss some more of the "how-to's."

I am sure that most of you have made lots and lots of introductions without even knowing it. The last time a friend came home with you after school and you said, "Mom, this is Jenny Jones," that was an introduction. Remember, always speak so that others can hear you and understand you when you do an introduction. Sometimes people mumble when they are nervous or unsure of what they are supposed to say. Think about what you are going to say before you say it, and you won't have any problems.

I can't think of anything about doing introductions that can put butterflies in your stomach faster than forgetting someone's name. Most people have had that happen to them, and they will all tell you that just being honest is the best bet. When it happens to me, I just say, "Please forgive me, but your name has slipped my memory." That's really the best you can do and most people will understand. Many times I have the mothers of my charm school students approach me in a shopping mall several years after their daughters have finished the class. I will probably remember their face, but unless they tell me whose mom they are, I will probably not recall their name. Be a good friend. Instead of standing there watching someone look for a hole to crawl into from embarrassment, help them out. I'm certain they will not forget your name again!

Basically, there are two ways to do introductions: formal and informal. The method you choose may depend on how old you are or where you are.

A sample of the informal way would be, "This is my friend, Jessica Rodrieguez." The same introduction done formally would be, "May I present my friend, Miss Jessica Rodrieguez." The fancy way might seem a little more grown-up, so make certain that the occasion calls for such an introduction. You wouldn't want your friends to think you are "putting on airs."

It is important to stand up when you are introducing or when you are being introduced. It not only shows respect, but shows that you are really interested in meeting the new friend. I always like to repeat the new person's name immediately. "Linda, I would like you to meet Cindy." It is helpful if I then say, "Cindy, it is so nice to meet you." Now I have had the chance to use her name while I am looking at her. It also helps some people to make a little mental picture in their mind of something about the new friend. We all have our own method to help us remember. There used to be page after page of strict rules for introducing new friends. If you stick to the basics, you won't have any problems. There are, however, some situations that may be a little more formal. Should you ever have the pleasure of meeting the President of the United States, you would say, "How do you do, Mr. President." If the special person was a king or queen, you would say, "How do you do, Your Majesty."

In the rare (and exciting!) case of meeting royalty, a curtsey would be appropriate for girls of all ages. A curtsey looks a little like a bow and a little like a dance step. If you are wearing a skirt or dress, you delicately hold the sides of your skirt between your thumb and index finger. Take your right foot and draw an imaginary half-circle with your toe until it is directly behind the heel of your left foot. Pretend that there is a bucket of water on your head. Now if you tip your head, you are not only going to get water all over you, but all over the queen! Practice in front of a mirror the next time you feel special.

Remember to smile not only when you are performing an introduction but when you are being introduced. It shows immediate friendship and will make the other person feel at ease instantly.

When a young lady of age twelve or older is introduced to an older man, it is appropriate for her to extend her hand. If you were being introduced to an older woman, you should wait for her to extend her hand to you. Young girls rarely shake hands with each other. When you are much older it would not only be acceptable but considered proper business etiquette.

You will want to address most adults as "Miss," "Mr.," or "Mrs." Some women prefer to be addressed as "Ms."

It is considered improper for a young person to be too casual or too familiar with an adult's name or title. You would not refer to a teacher by his or her first name even if it were a teacher you felt especially close to.

Adults with special titles, jobs or positions are sometimes introduced or referred to in a special way.

The Mayor: "How do you do, Mr. Mayor" or "How do you do, Mayor Jones."

The Rabbi: "How do you do, Rabbi Gould" or "How do you do, Rabbi."

Protestant Minister: "How do you do, Rev. Womble" or "How do you do, Sir."

Catholic Priest: "How do you do, Father O'Malley" or "How do you do, Father."

Nun: "How do you do, Sister" or "How do you do, Sister Bernadette."

The Governor: "How do you do, Governor Mayfield."

His Wife: "How do you do, Mrs. Mayfield."

A Senator: "How do you do, Senator Dempsey" or "How do you do, Senator."

Introducing a boy to a girl—say the girl's name first:

"Suzy Kelly, this is Patrick O'Reilly."

Introducing a boy to your sister—look first at your sister and say her name:

"Tina, this is Paul Reese."

Then look back at your sister and say "Tina's my sister."

Introducing a friend to your mother—a boy looks at his mom and says her name first:

"Mom, this is Ashley Brookes."

Introducing a man to a woman—You say the woman's name first:

"Mrs. Kemp, this is Mr. James."

Introducing a person your age to an older person—you say the older person's name first:

"Mr. Potter, this is Sarah Smith."

Introducing any boy to your dad—say your dad's name first:

"Dad, this is Jamie Jones."

Introducing a school-age girl to your dad—look first at your dad and say his name:

"Dad, this is Angela Morsam."

Introducing your brother to a boy—you look first at your friend and say his name:

"Andrew Jones, this is my brother Tim."

Conversation

Conversation is defined very simply as, "the act of more than one person discussing a single topic or more than one topic with one another."

The last time you called one of your schoolmates and talked about what a surprise the math quiz was today, you had a conversation. A conversation is normally based on a pleasant subject. Sometimes, grown-ups just call it "chitchat." It is light and easy, usually.

An argument, on the other hand, is also a conversation, only not very pleasant. It is a conversation between two people on a subject with which they disagree.

A conversation is certainly more pleasant than an argument, but none of us is going to go through life without a few conflicts or disagreements. Loud talking and fussing is not conversation. When you are upset about something, you should wait until you are alone with the person or persons who made you feel that way. Having someone confront you in the hall at school when all your friends are there is very embarrassing and will, most likely, cause even more hostility. Anger is what turns conversation into confrontation. Usually, people who are insecure become boisterous around others. Perhaps they are in need of attention. Have you ever noticed that sometimes the kids in school who most often get in trouble and act up in class are the same kids who are really shy and in need of a true friend deep down inside?

Occasionally, someone will try to get the upper hand or act like a bully, or maybe even get on the defensive when you approach them only because they do not have the self-confidence that it would take to explain their point calmly.

One of the easiest math exercises you will ever learn is that "Two wrongs never make a right!" Be as calm as you can be whenever you are explaining your opinions. You do not ever want to be accused of being difficult or hard to get along with.

Now, don't misunderstand. It is perfectly acceptable to disagree with someone if you are certain that you can do it without being bossy. No one likes a "Little Miss Know-it-All." There is nothing wrong with expressing your own ideas or standing up for what you think is right.

The tone of your voice has a lot to do with how your friends, family, and acquaintances will react to what you say. If you try to make a point or state your ideas about something in a loud voice, everyone might think that you are ready to argue. If you are in a group and everyone is trying to make a point at the same time, it is really tempting to talk louder so that everyone can hear what you have to say. Resist the urge to do that. Sit back patiently and wait your turn to talk. When you do talk, use a soft, but confident voice. You know what I do when I'm in a group and everyone is trying to talk at once? I walk away and lose interest in what they *all* have to say!

We've discussed a little of what conversation is, but now let's discuss some of what it shouldn't be.

Too Personal. Stay away from questions like "How much money do your parents make?," "Why don't you live in a bigger house?" and "Why does your dad drive that old car?" Think about how embarrassed you would be if someone asked you that kind of question! Now, I didn't say that questions were taboo. Quite the contrary. Questions are probably the very best way to get a conversation going; it is the *type* of question you ask that makes the difference.

Instead, try something like, "You must be new in the neighborhood. Where did you live before?" Or, certainly one of the easiest ones for you would be "What school do you go to?" or "Did you take a vacation this summer?"

Just remember, always try to put yourself in the place of the person being asked the question. If it is something that you would not feel comfortable being asked, then they probably won't either.

Unpleasant Subjects. It's one thing to talk about a biology experiment if you are with a group of your friends in the same project. But I wouldn't recommend it if you are having dinner with your friends' parents. Generally, dinner-time is not a great time to discuss such subjects as parts of the body and how they work, the horribly gross accident you heard about on the way home, or someone's very sad news.

Subjects such as upcoming school projects, new friends you made, church activities, or hobbies are much more acceptable. The same rule applies here that applies in almost all other cases—if it's a subject that you would not want to hear about, maybe others wouldn't either.

Too Fast or Too Slow. Trying to pay attention to someone who is talking "a mile a minute" is not only annoying, but frustrating. A person who talks too fast sounds nervous; when a person sounds nervous when speaking, we sometimes tend to question the value of what they have to say. You may find yourself chattering away if you are very excited. If you just won the girl's relay race for your whole school, or made the chorus, you have every right to be excited. Just remember to take your time and speak clearly.

Being around someone who speaks too slowly is just as annoying. Have you ever sat patiently while a friend dragged on and on with a somewhat boring conversation? You wouldn't want to hurt your friend's feelings for the world, but you begin to wonder how much longer you can sit and be attentive. What do you do? You may do one of two things; first, you can sit quietly and be as patient as possible, or if you have a great deal of self-confidence and timing, you can slip in a question about the subject to show your friend that you are not only paying attention but that you can hardly wait until they finish their exciting story!

Me, Me, Me! Speaking of boring subjects! Folks who only know how to talk about their own accomplishments tend to get boring and annoying very quickly. They take over a conversation telling about all of the wonderful things they have done. I have found from experience that if someone is really that great, you will more than likely hear about it from another source.

Being proud of something you have done is perfectly all right. In fact, it's great! Just resist the temptation to talk only of what you have done and leave out your other friends. It's alright to say "I just won the spelling bee for my class for the third year in a row! Do you enjoy spelling, Jennie?" This way you bring your friends into the conversation instead of leaving them on the sidelines listening to how wonderful you are!

You will receive many more compliments if you follow those rules. A compliment is such a pleasant gift. It makes you feel proud inside for knowing that your hard work paid off—somebody noticed! Give compliments freely. It doesn't cost a penny and you will make someone feel so special.

Introvert or Extrovert? Which one are you? You're probably asking what in the world they mean. Let's take the word introvert first. The prefix of this word is *intro*; the first syllable is *in*. People who are introverts stay into themselves. They do not tend to speak up very much. Sometimes, introverts are very shy. However, sometimes an introvert is just very cautious about what they say and how they say it. When they speak, you usually listen. Their words are weighed very carefully.

An extrovert, on the other hand, is just the opposite. They are bubbly, outgoing, and tend to turn strangers into acquaintances with ease.

Is there a right or wrong way to be? Not really, since both traits have their good and bad points. An introvert may miss out on making new friends, voicing an opinion, or being included in social activities. An extrovert might be so busy talking that she forgets to be a good listener. What is right is what's right for you. If you are perfectly content being an extrovert, and you will allow yourself the ability to include and listen to your friends, and you do not come on too strong, then enjoy your gregarious personality.

If an introvert is secretly wishing she could walk to the other side of the room and introduce herself to new friends but cannot because of the butterflies in her tummy, then she needs to practice some conversation skills. (Always taking a friend with you helps, too.)

Personality
Exercise #1

List your attributes below. (These are the things you like best about yourself.)

The Outer You (Physical Appearance) Ex: good posture	The Inner You (Personality) Ex: nice voice
I have lots of friends and run very fast.	I think I am funny, pretty, and good at babysitting.

Now, I am certain that most of you hesitated in filling this out. My students throughout the years *always* have. Remember, there is a difference between self-confidence and conceit. Feeling good about yourself is a very special part of your jigsaw puzzle.

If you'll think of yourself sort of like a jigsaw puzzle, it will help you to form a "picture" in your head of what the Total You should be like—the Pretty You! Here are some ideas for your puzzle pieces:

— The way you talk
— The way you look
— The way you think
— The way you feel/emotion
— The way you walk
— The way you behave

You do not have to be a certain age, height, weight, nationality, or "look" to be popular and charming. What comes to your mind when I say the word "charming?" Is it that secret sense of knowing what to do and when? Do you know girls who always seem to do the right thing at the right time while you shuffle around awkwardly? The answer is probably yes, not necessarily because you *are* awkward but because you may lack the confidence and positive self-image it takes to be confident.

Personality
Exercise #2

Decorate an empty shoe box in a collage that best describes you. A collage is a group of pictures or illustrations. Make sure you cut up only magazines or catalogs that have mom's approval. You can use anything you like. Glue the pictures all over the outside of the box until you have "packaged" yourself. Decorate the lid separately so that you can open and close the box easily. You will be using the box for other projects later in your book.

(Fun project—get a few friends together when you do your box. See if you recognize each other's.)

Being Popular

If there was a magic pill that you could take to make you the most popular girl in your school, would you take it? Your answer is probably a very emphatic "Yes!" My dears, that just simply does not exist, but I am certain that many girls have wished for such a pill since time began. Popularity seems to be the main goal for many girls, more important sometimes than good grades. Being in the "right crowd" at school certainly can seem like the ultimate goal. But will it really assure you of happiness and success?

When I was still in school, I wanted that popularity worse than anything. I was a chubby little kid who didn't always get picked for the kick-ball team. Imagine how you would feel if the teacher had to make a team take you! Sure, I cried on the way home from school more than once. I thought that nobody would ever really like me. Well, you know—the right people. My parents meant well, but the best advice they could give me was to be honest, nice, and always be a loyal friend. Some help that was, I thought. I figured the other kids would think I was so nerdy that any hopes of them ever accepting me would be destroyed. It was bad enough that I was smart and that the teacher liked me! Well, at that point in my young life, I figured the worst thing that would happen if I tried this was that I would be ignored. Okay, worth a try!

It worked! My life seemed to have a new beginning! When I was happy and friendly it seemed to be contagious. The kids who thought that I couldn't possibly be normal and fun got a real surprise. Now, that doesn't mean that they were right for not playing with me because I was a chubby, possibly nerdy, teacher's pet kind of kid, but what it does mean is that it takes two to start a friendship. It has continued to work for me to this day. It is almost impossible not to smile back when someone flashes you a happy grin!

Not everyone can be a cheerleader or the class president. Find the special things that you do best and enjoy the most. Become a master of those things and do not dwell on the things that are not your specialty. Concentrate on being the very best YOU that you can be!

Popularity. If it makes you feel any better, even the popular girls have moments of insecurity. Absolutely *everyone* has felt as though they could crawl in a hole and die.

What do you notice about the people who seem to possess popularity and a sense of ease? Let's discuss a few. Add a few of your own if you think of others.

Sense of Humor. My personal favorite and, without a doubt, this is the one trait that has helped me out of potentially embarrassing situations. Appreciate others and look for things to laugh about—especially yourself! Learn to laugh *with* people, not at them.

Good Relationships. Having a mutual respect for your parents, siblings, step-brothers, step-sisters, and step-parents. Always allow them the same courtesy that you expect.

Appreciate Beautiful Things. There is beauty all around you. Learn to notice it frequently. It can be very simple—a flower, the coo of a new baby, a special friend, freshly mown grass. Nature gives us so many wonderful things to cherish. Don't waste all of this beauty! It's yours for the taking.

Healthy Emotions. To express sincere, spontaneous surprise, joy, happiness, even sorrow, should come naturally. When an emotion is too staged or dramatic, it will be obvious.

Be an Interesting Friend. Although it's always easier to talk about things that are familiar to you, you must also practice the ability to listen and learn about those around you. You may be pleasantly surprised at the wonderful knowledge you may gain from others.

Caring and Graciousness. Be kind to others in your heart. Refrain from gossip and jokes at the expense of others. Try not to be stingy with praise and compliments.

Self-Confidence. Believe in yourself. Do daily mental exercises to boost your self-esteem. We all need an occasional boost to the spirit. If you truly practice "If you can believe it, you can achieve it," you will not be disappointed!

While we are on the subject of popularity and getting along with others, I would like to share some valuable information with you. First of all, I have always been a big sister to my many students over the years. Although I am a mother myself, I tend to hear a lot of things from my students that perhaps they would not feel comfortable telling their own moms. If you are ever asked to do something that you not believe in or agree with just for the sake of being popular, please stop, think, and remember that following your head as well as following your heart are usually excellent guidelines. As you get older, you will never regret your good judgment.

Manners Don't Go Out of Style

Consider how important your life is. Think about your future. Remember that being smart is part of being pretty, and being the very best you possible.

At times you may feel that having good manners, obeying rules, and being a charming young lady are not "cool." There is no easy way to prove these things to each of you. It takes a great deal of trust. Hopefully, it is the trust in your family and especially the trust in yourself, that will ease the transition of growing up.

When you are a "Pretty Me" on the inside, you cannot help but be a "Pretty Me" on the outside.

Telephone Etiquette

There is no doubt that the telephone will be a constant companion to you throughout your life. As a student, its use will enable you to catch up on homework; as an employee, it may be crucial to your daily responsibilities; as a parent, it may help you arrange a surprise birthday party for your daughter! As a young girl growing up, it may seem like a physical addition to your body!

Have you ever had a grown-up ask you if the phone was permanently attached to your face? Depending on how many people share the telephone in your home, your parents may set down some livable guidelines.

If your parents conduct business from home, your telephone time may be limited. Some families have separate telephone lines for the kids in the household. Most people, however, do not enjoy such a luxury.

Your personal phone calls may be limited to five or ten minutes and may also be limited to certain times during the day or evening. Please adhere to the rules for telephone use in your home.

Each family will have their own way to properly answer the phone. I will suggest a few ways to you, but always clear these procedures with your family first.

If you have older brothers and sisters, the telephone is probably used a lot around your house. In fact, you may sometimes get frustrated when you feel it is your turn for telephone privileges.

Sharing and understanding is the name of the game. You can set up a a telephone use chart similar to the one you may have done for the bathroom.

Your family may wish for you to answer the phone by saying your family surname (last name). For example, "Hello, Morgan residence." They may even wish you to add your name at the end of this type of greeting. "Hello, Taylor residence, Judi speaking."

Just saying "Hello" in a pleasant voice is certainly adequate. If you are home alone for any reason and are allowed to answer the telephone, it may be wise not to state your name.

Although most people in the world are kind and honest, there may be people with illnesses or problems that cause them to call homes where children and teens are alone and frighten them. If you are home alone after school or at any other time, you need to be very careful who you offer information to. If someone calls asking for your mom or dad and you do not recognize the voice as being a friend or family member, simply ask who is calling, state that the parent or other grown-up is "in the shower," "taking a nap," or perhaps, "busy and can't come to the phone right now." Ask for the caller's name and phone number and tell them that your parent will call them back shortly.

The Written Word

There will be many occasions in your life when you will need to write a note or a letter. How many can you name?

Thank You Notes   Invitations
Business Letters   Friendly Letters
Notes of Condolence   Memorandums

You may think of others later.

Most of the correspondence that you write now will be hand written, however, you may wish to use a typewriter or a computer as you get older (or busier).

A young lady's handwriting says a lot about her. It can very well be an indication of how careful and cautious, how well groomed and neat, how meticulous and, even how organized she is. Wow! I'll bet you never thought of all that when you did your homework last night!

In the *Treasure* section of this book, you will have an opportunity to practice your handwriting. As you record all of the wonderful things that are happening to you, you'll want to make certain that you have used the very best example of your handwriting.

With just a very few exceptions, all of the people that I know who have sloppy handwriting also need to practice their neatness in other ways.

Thank-You Notes. I hope you'll need to write many of these in your life! Writing a thank-you note is appropriate whenever you receive a gift or a nice gesture from someone. Birthdays, graduations, weddings—any special occasion when someone would receive a gift—even Christmas and Chanukah would be a lovely idea (after all, you are receiving gifts). A thank-you note should be handwritten on a note card. Some people like to use a printed note card with "Thank You" on the front. I prefer to buy plain note cards in a pretty pastel color so that I can use them for other types of notes. That way, I always have the right kind of note card available. If someone happens to surprise me with a gift, I can sit

41

right down and prepare my thank-you note!

Don't forget to write a nice note if you have been someone's house guest. What a special gift that is! If you have been an overnight guest for a weekend or more, a small gift is appropriate. (More on house guesting later.)

Letters. Communicating with people on paper is to write a letter. It costs less than long distance phone calls and can be fun and creative as well. Write a letter very naturally, just the way you would talk.

There are a few simple rules to remember when writing:

1.
January 1, 1989

2.
Dear Marci,

3.

4. Love,
Jessica

1. **Date**—Goes in the upper corner of your paper
2. **Salutation**—The greeting line of your letter is placed above the body of the letter: Dear Josey, Dear Mr. Andersen.
3. **Body**—This is your opportunity to "speak" in your letter. Use proper grammar and keep your dictionary and thesaurus close by. If your letter is neatly done and well planned, the person receiving it will think highly of you. Get in the habit of writing nice, neat, interesting letters,

even if they are only for chit-chat among friends. As you grow older, the letter writing skills you will have acquired will benefit you greatly.

4. **The Closing**—Is normally "Love," or "Affectionately," if it is a close friend or family member, but "Yours truly," or "Sincerely," would be appropriate for a more casual acquaintance.

5. **The Envelope**—Make sure your envelope is addressed properly. Don't start the address up so high that there won't be room for the postage stamp, and please don't forget your complete return address just in case anything goes wrong and your letter needs to be returned to you.

Remember, letters and notes are like conversations—only on paper.

Chapter II
Being Pretty

I know that a lot of you will skip around in your book and read the parts that interest you most. Many of you have probably turned to this chapter because everyone likes to be pretty. There are few subjects as exciting and interesting to young girls everywhere as beauty. Looking our best allows us to feel better about everything that we do, whether it's feeling comfortable in new situations or just going to school each day. Looking your best gives you the constant flow of self-confidence needed to be the *very best you* you can be and isn't that really what you want?

Let's start at the top of your head and work down to skin care, teeth, nails, and dressing well, and of course, we'll talk about your constant companion—your figure!

Hair

Your "crowning glory," halo, frame for your lovely face, mop, scraggly mess . . . . Has your hair ever been described like any of these? If your hair looks great, so does your whole face, and if it doesn't—well, it just makes you feel unkept and ill-groomed.

The nicest thing you can do for your hair is keep it clean. Shampooing once a week may be enough for your hair and scalp, or you may need to shampoo daily. The key is to do what's right for you. When you hair begins to "separate" at the roots and look heavy or oily, it's time for a shampoo. Other girls can tell that their hair is dirty because it hangs limp and flat to their head. You'll know when it's time. Mother may still need to help you when you wash your hair, especially rinsing.

Not everyone's hair puts out such an easy "signal" like looking oily when it gets dirty, so let's talk about different types of hair and how to care for them properly.

Oily Hair

Looks like:

— Separates and sometimes looks darker at roots (especially on light hair).

— Feels heavy and looks limp when dirty

What to do:

— Never wash your hair in hot water, always warm; then rinse in cool water to close pores in scalp. Hair will be shinier and cleaner!

— Lather two or three times if needed.

— Use a shampoo for oily hair.

— Use conditioner or creme rinse from your ear level down only.

Special help:

— If your hair is long, learn how to wear it up in French braids or clever off-the-neck hairstyles, especially in warm weather.

— Make sure ends are trimmed every six to eight weeks.

Dry hair

Looks like:

— Usually has split ends.

— Not very shiny.

— If it's very damaged, it can look like straw.

— Can look bushy if it's thick.

What to do:

— Use a shampoo for dry or damaged hair.

— Use a creme rinse for tangles.
— Avoid over-exposure to sun, wind and blow dryers.

Special help:
—"Extra help" conditioner twice a month.
—Trim split ends every 6-8 weeks.

Flat Hair
Looks like:
—Thin, limp.
— Fly-away look.
— Baby fine.

What to do:
— Shampoo with gentle pH balanced product.
— Use protein conditioner.
— Keep ends evenly trimmed; the blunter the cut, the thicker the hair will look.

Special help:
— Stay away from creme rinses that soften and flatten hair.
— Keep hair above shoulder length.
— Lean over with head upside down if blow-drying; this makes hair appear fuller. A little hair spray for special occasions helps.
— Consider a body perm for fullness and shape.

Coarse, Curly or Kinky

Looks like:
— Thick and wiry.
— Curly.
— Unruly or out of control.
— Often appears dry and bushy.

What to do:
— Shampoo once or twice a week.
— Avoid dampness and humidity that causes the frizzies.
— Keep hair trimmed and thinned to remove excess bulk.

Special help:
— Avoid heat appliances such as blow dryers, hot rollers, and curling irons.
— Have hair cut into a "wash-and-go" style.
— Do not attempt straightening kits for extremely curly or kinky hair at home; have this professionally done.
— Avoid allowing hair to become too long and out of control.
— Master the excitement and fun of braids and hair ornaments.

Normal Hair

Looks like:
— Shiny and healthy.
— Bouncy.
— Not too oily, not too dry.

What to do:
— Shampoo when needed.
— Creme rinse for tangles and deep conditioner as needed
— Rinse well, using cool water.
— Trim every six to eight weeks as needed.

Special help:
— Just because your hair is normal now, don't get lazy and over-expose to heat appliances and sunlight.

Some Hair Care Do's and Don't's

Do	Don't
Use a wide-tooth plastic comb for detangling wet hair.	Brush hair when wet; it stretches and breaks.
Drink plenty of milk and water to keep hair shiny and bouncy.	Eat junk food and not expect the ill-effects to show up in your hair.
Remove barrettes, pins, and other ornaments when sleeping.	Use real rubber bands in hair ever; only coated types.
Use a shampoo that's right for you.	Use handfuls of shampoo; a fifty-cent-piece sized dollop is plenty.
Use a fresh, clean towel to dry your hair.	Use a blow dryer without an adult's permission.
Wear a hairstyle that fits your lifestyle.	Use an electric heat appliance near water.
Keep hair out of eyes.	Leave the house with wet hair in cold weather.
Wash brushes and combs every two weeks.	Comb hair at mealtime.
	Ever cut your own hair or a friend's; same goes for perms, relaxers, etc.

Just For Fun. Cut out a picture of the hairstyle that you think would make you like a million bucks and tape it below. Are you in need of a new look—or just something easier?

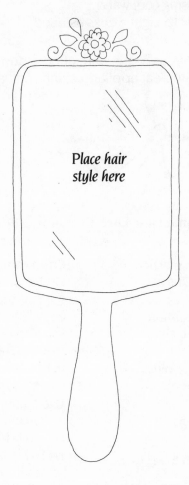

Place hair
style here

Now, answer the following questions about the style you selected:
— Does the person in the picture have the same color hair as me?
— Does the person have the same type of hair—curly, straight, limp?
— Does the style require more time than you are willing to give before the school bus comes?

Sometimes, we see pretty pictures of models or actresses in magazines or catalogs and wish we could look like them. Remember that the cute, pixie-faced red head's curly bob will not look the same on the sweet, pale blonde with stick straight locks!

Adults have a saying for this—"The grass is always greener on the other side of the fence." It's the truth. I've rarely met a girl with naturally curly hair who didn't at some point wish it were poker straight and vice-versa.

Learn to work with what you've got. Ask Mother to take you to a reputable hair salon that is used to working with young girls. An experienced stylist can be honest and realistic when helping you pick out a style. Even very young girls take care of their hair differently now than just a few years ago. Many hairstyles require sprays, spritzes, gel, mousses, and an assortment of clips and appliances. Gone are the days when anyone younger than your mom simply wore her hair in a traditional pony tail or braids. But remember, keep it simple. You don't need lots of extra foo-foo at your age. All the extras can sometimes take away from your healthy "crowning glory"—and that wonderful face of yours!

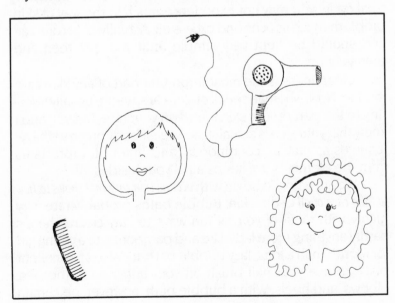

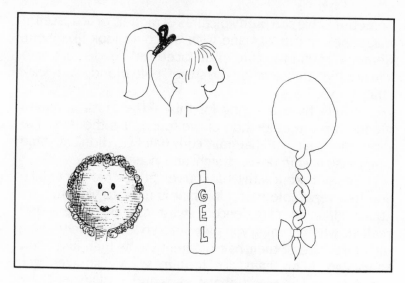

Skin Deep

As you'll see in the nutrition chapter, beauty really is a lot more than skin deep, but your skin certainly is a very visible subject to discuss.

Until you are old enough to begin your monthly menstrual cycle, you may not experience much in the way of skin problems such as acne and excess oil. Actually, skin care can and should be kept very simple until your pre-teen and teen years.

Cleanliness is the most important part of any skin care routine. Now, when we speak of skin care, we are usually referring to the part of your skin found on your face. But you and I know that your skin is actually the largest body organ we have. It serves as our "air conditioner" and "filter." It protects us from the elements *and* keeps all of your insides in!

We are going to begin with *over all skin care that shows us how to take care of all* of our skin. Bubble baths probably rate very highly with most of you for fun ways to stay clean. There's hardly anything more lady-like and pampering to a young girl (or Mom!) than a long, lazy bubble bath. It's also an excellent place to use your nail brush on your finger nails, toenails, elbows, and heels. With a bubble bath, however, be certain to rinse off all the soap thoroughly so that your skin does not become irritated.

When you get out of the tub, smooth on an after-bath lotion. Apply it while skin is still warm and slightly damp. Since you should not be wearing perfume until your early teen years, now is a good time to fluff on lots of wonderful baby powder!

If you're like most girls, you will need to choose a shower over a bath most of the time because showers take less time. It may just be too hectic around your house before school to take a bubble bath and tie up the bathroom for the needed amount of time. (After all, you shouldn't rush a bubble bath!) Choose one night per week for your special session—maybe Saturdays.

Facial Skin Care. There's no doubt that the portion of skin we all pay more attention to is under our hairline. That's right. It's that great face of yours! It is unique to you, and no one can be exactly like you.

Skin care for your face does not need to be complicated when you are young and have not begun wearing make-up on a regular basis. When you take your daily bath or shower, you may also wash your face. A good habit to establish would be setting aside a different wash cloth or sponge just for your face and neck. *Actually*, a clean wash cloth should be used each time you wash your face, but your mother will probably scream when you tell her this. Solution: offer to wash and dry them yourself or use a facial sponge instead. Because the sponge is porous and dries quickly, germs and bacteria do not have an opportunity to grow. That's when you run into skin problems. Wash cloths normally get balled up (still drippy) and stuck in the corner of the bath tub. Then, while you're at school, they get warm and smelly—just the ideal environment for a new crop of "beasties" to jump back on your face next time you wash. Yuk!

The different skin types are similar to the different hair types: normal, oily, dry, combination, and problem. Remember that if you are under twelve or thirteen, you may not notice a certain "type" of skin yet. Just keeping it clean is the most important thing to do. Wash in the morning and again before bedtime using gentle circular motions with your cloth or sponge and a facial soap or cleansing solution.

It is important to know what type of skin you have so

that you can take care of it properly and so you know what kind of make-up to choose when the time comes.

Normal Skin
- Not too dry, not too oily.
- Pores (your skin's "breathing holes") are practically invisible.
- Not overly sensitive to products.
- Cleanse with mild soap morning and night; rinse and pat dry with clean towel.
- In cold weather, moisturize with a light lotion or cold cream on any exposed skin to avoid wind burn and chapping.

Oily Skin
— Surface sometimes shiny with blackheads, pimples, and large pores.

— Wash with medicated soap morning and evening. Rinse with warm water, then cool; pat dry.

— If needed, apply mild astringent in T-zone (across forehead, down to nose, and including chin); also, place on any other breakout points.

— Never squeeze or pop a pimple; you can cause a scar and scars are forever. General rule is: don't pick at your face ever!

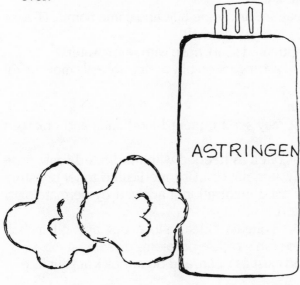

— Apply light, non-oily moisturizer on flaky areas or if skin dries out in cold weather.

Dry Skin
— Feels tight shortly after washing.
— May sunburn easily.
— Flakes and chaps easily.
— Wash with creamy soap or gentle cleanser morning and night. Rinse thoroughly since leftover soap dries skin; pat dry.
— Moisturize with non-oily, light weight cream morning and night; carry a sample size bottle with you for extra help during the day if needed.

Combination Skin
— Some areas are dry, some oily, and some normal (T-zone is oily, rest is dry or normal).
— Cleanse with mild soap, rinse with warm water.
— Apply mild astringent on oily areas, non-oily moisturizer to others.

Problem Skin
— Often oily, may see frequent blackheads and enlarged pores.
— Cleanse as often as needed with medicated soap, rinse with cool water; pat dry. Use medicated toner or astringent. Use acne medication if advised by dermatologist (skin doctor).
— Keep hair "squeaky" clean since dirt and oil in hair around face can increase problems on skin.
— Keep hands just as clean, and do not pick at your face.

A Word About Our Glorious Sunshine. Beware soft skinned beauties! Yes, *you*. This warning applies to each and every one of you. Those wonderful, warm, lazy days of summer seem to call us to the beach for sun and frolic—and no one will disagree with the fun factor! Just remember that even on a cloudy day the ultraviolet rays from the sun can beam down through the clouds and give you a nasty burn.

Your skin production of *melanin*—a pigment released into the skin to naturally protect you from the sun—determines how easily you will tan. Too much of a good thing can be harmful.

Ask Mother if you should apply a sunscreen creme when you're outside playing. A sunscreen protects your skin and allows you to stay outside longer. If the sunscreen says that it has an SPF-8 (sun protection factor), you can wear it and stay outside eight times longer than with no protection. If you are very fair skinned, you may want to use a total sun block which does not allow any of the ultraviolet rays through. Remember that you will need to reapply the sunscreen product if you're playing hard or just coming out of the pool or ocean.

A healthy glow in the summer may be pretty, but be smart and protect yourself.

Your skin will probably change several times as you grow older. Typically, our skin is normal when we're very young, starts to get oily into our pre-teen and teen years, may be problem prone in our teens, continues to change and become combination in our twenties and thirties and will probably become fairly dry as we become much older.

Our Beauty Routine. A *routine* is a plan that you follow for something that you do regularly. Do you have a routine in the morning to help you get ready for school? Those of you who do probably find that you spend less time running around in circles trying to decide what to do next. Your routine may be one for bed time, one for morning or both.

Writing something down really seems to help us remember how important it is to keep the commitment or the promise to ourselves to do the routine each day and night. Write down your routine below:

Morning	Bedtime
1.	1.
2.	2.
3.	3.
4.	4.
5.	5.

Add more if needed.

I think you'll be happy with how much a routine can help you feel organized. You will use a routine list for other important things, too. I've done one since I was a little girl, and I still do one every night before I go to bed which includes any little extra things I need to do for my family or errands I need to run.

I used to think it was silly for my mom to put lotion on my face before I left for school in the winter. I walked to and from school and played outside every day, especially when it snowed! She got me started on a smart skin care routine even when I was very young, and if you will do the same thing, you'll have skin that will be the envy of all your friends!

One last note on skin care. You might get a haircut that you don't like, and although you'll be unhappy, it's not the end of the world because your hair will grow. If you don't take good care of your skin right now, and you don't continue to spend the extra few minutes now and then to make sure it's extra clean and soft, you'll really regret it when you're a teenager.

Do's and Don't's

Do	Don't
Bathe or shower daily.	Poke at pimples.
Decide what "recipe" your skin and hair need.	Brush wet hair.
Plan a beauty routine and practice it regularly.	Wash your face with dirty wash cloths.
Have your own special place for good grooming treasures. Use the "Personality Box" you made earlier.	"Fry" your skin in the sun. Use regular rubber bands on hair.
Notice any changes in your hair or skin.	Use your teeth to open things.
Keep long hair pulled back in warm weather for comfort.	Put astringents on dry skin. Go out on a cold, windy day with an uprotected face.

Nails and Teeth

Nail Care. The special routine used for keeping your fingernails in tip-top shape is called a *manicure*. It's loads of fun to do (with mom's permission, of course) and is a special way to pamper yourself.

You will need the following items:

1. Clear polish
2. Cotton balls
3. Cuticle remover
4. Emery board
5. Fingernail brush
6. Hand lotion
7. Liquid soap

8. Nail clippers
9. Nail polish remover
10. Orange stick
11. Paper towel
12. Small bowl
13. Small hand towel

So that you can keep track of your manicure items, decorate a shoe box to match your dresser or bathroom and place the items in it. Don't have an adult do all the work, but please ask permission before using scissors, tape, and paste. Have fun doing this box because it also tells something about you. Are you frilly, out-doorsy, or ultra-modern? Lot's of things may show up when you're feeling artistic, you know!

1. Remove old polish.
2. File dry nails with smooth side of emery board to oval shape. Never file wet nails. Make certain that nails are not too pointed or squared and that they are kept fairly short (especially for girls under age thirteen).
3. Soak fingers (up to first knuckle) in warm, soapy water. Better yet, take a bubble bath and let the bath water work wonders on any hardened cuticles. *Cuticles* are the tough or hard skin that grows up around the area where your nail grows and your skin leaves off. It doesn't really do any harm except to be just as tempting for nervous chewing as your fingernails can sometimes be! It also makes your nails appear shorter.
4. Gently push back dampened cuticle with the blunt end of your orange stick. No, the stick is not orange in color but made from the wood of an orange tree. It does not easily splinter and is very soft, making it perfect for working near the delicate skin surrounding your nails. *Hang nails* are the ragged little pieces of skin that mysteriously appear just below your fingernails practically overnight! Do not bite them since they can be *very* painful. If one of these painful little skin tabs pops up on you, clip it carefully with your nail clippers soaked in alcohol, and then apply a drop of antiseptic. (You may need an adult's help.)
5. For stubborn cuticle areas, go back and use cuticle remover.
6. Gently scrub nails with nail brush and check for any stubborn dirt with slanted end of orange stick.
7. Dry nails with towel.
8. Resting your hand on a clean paper towel, brush on one clear coat of nail polish. Make it very thin and take care not to allow polish to touch your skin. If it does, simply wrap a little cotton around the end of your orange stick, dip in polish remover, and use as a cotton swab to remove boo-boos.
9. Let nails dry at least ten minutes before applying hand lotion.
10. For older girls who are using a neutral polish, apply two

coats of color after the clear polish since it now serves as a base coat. When color has dried for fifteen to twenty minutes, apply another coat of clear as a protective top coat. A little extra clear polish on underside of nail tip keeps color from wearing off as quickly.

There you have it—a beautiful set of fingernails to be proud of! As well groomed as they are now, even the most dedicated nail biter would have second thoughts!

Remember, these steps can be repeated for your toenails, and we call it a *pedicure*. Wouldn't a hand decorated "coupon" presented to your mother for a manicure and pedicure to be done by you be a special treat?

Let's point our beautiful fingers at a few last **do's** and **don't's.**

Do	Don't
Rub baby cream or baby oil onto cuticle area before going to bed.	Wear dark or bright nail colors for school or before teen years.
Apply only thin coats of polish.	Wear decals, charms and glitter.
Allow nails to dry before going to bed.	Bite your nails! It doesn't just look bad, but you'll swallow germs.
Use hair dryer to dry nails fast, but no closer than 12 inches. (Remember,always get an adult's permission for using appliances.)	Use metal nail files.
	Allow polish to chip half-way off before removing for good.
Place cotton balls between your toes before polishing.	Use your nails as a "tool;" they will break.
Wear shoes that fit properly to avoid painful foot conditions.	Allow several different lengths of nails if they begin to break.

That Dazzling Smile. There are few things more pleasant than the smile on a young girl's face. Make sure yours is healthy by following these tips:

— Visit your dentist regularly.
— Avoid sugary snacks; learn to love fruits and raw vegetables.

— Brush after each meal. If you cannot brush at school, eat a raw apple or celery to dislodge hiding food particles. Swishing water around in your mouth can loosen food particles, too.
— Floss teeth before each brushing to make sure nothing's hiding and to keep gums healthy.
— Brush in an up-and-down motion, remembering inside surfaces as well as back teeth.
— Get plenty of calcium (see nutrition section).
— Once a week, brush with a mixture of one teaspoon of baking soda mixed with one teaspoon of salt. This removes stains and makes teeth glow! It's worth the taste.
— Don't pick at your teeth with pens, combs, etc.
— Never use your teeth as a tool to open hair pins or packages.
— Don't forget to brush your gums.
— Don't be ashamed of braces; just think of the beautiful smile you will soon have.

Dressing Well

The art of dressing well for young girls used to be pretty simple. You wore frilly party dresses and white gloves to birthday parties and church, jumpers or skirts and sweaters to school, and play clothes (pants and such) were strictly for the playground when school was out.

Well, you know it's not that simple any more. You have your own sense of style and your personality shines through with each outfit you choose. You may still enjoy the frilly things and the ever popular classics like skirts and sweaters, but there's another side of you who may want to dress a little more grown-up at times, sort of up-beat and fun.

You were not allowed to wear pants or shorts in my elementary school. It got a little cold walking to school in the winter, so we were allowed to wear pants under our skirts or dresses. We took them off and put them in our "cubbies" during the school day, but we certainly looked silly traveling to and from school!

You have so many pretty pants outfits to choose from

now that unless you have to wear skirts or uniforms to school, you can stay comfortable and warm, *plus* be in style and look super! (Please note, if you wear pants to school, it doesn't mean it's okay to sit like a boy at your desk!)

It doesn't really matter how many clothes you have or what name brand they are but it is how you wear them that truly counts.

A girl can wear an expensive designer outfit but have messy hair, dirty nails, and poor posture. Being a fashion snob is silly and immature. Some people can afford to spend lots of money on their clothes and some cannot, but this has absolutely nothing to do with how much fun they can be or how good a friend they will be. Remember this, and you will always be the special young lady you are now.

Have you ever thought about why we wear clothes? Can you list some of the reasons why you think we wear clothes?

We'd be naked, cold, i'mbearist, and funny looking.

65

Here's a few. Did you have any of the same ones?

1. To protect your body from the elements—rain, heat, snow, etc.
2. To make us more attractive.
3. So we don't get arrested in public!
4. Because it's fun.

Let's Get Organized. This will probably be your mom's favorite part of the book—organizing your closet and dresser drawers! It's not as bad as it sounds; it can actually be sort of fun.

Let's begin by taking everything out of your closet and piling it on the floor (clean floor, of course). Start by making neat piles on your bed of things that are the same—pants together, blouses together, and so on. Then, hang them in your closet the same way. Be sure not to double up clothes on one hanger because you'll have such a hard time finding that favorite shirt when you're running late for school! If you're really clever, try hanging each category by color as well.

Now it's time for dresser drawers. (The very thought may frighten some of you.) I'll tell you from experience that you'll be better off dumping them (one at a time, please) on your bed and go from there. You should have one sock drawer, one underwear drawer, and so on. If you have just a small amount of one particular thing, you can use one drawer for two things. Maybe hair barrettes and t-shirts can share a space.

Helpful hint—Cut shoe boxes so that they are one-half inch shorter than the top of your drawers, arrange inside and use to keep things from running together. For items that need more room, ask Mother for some empty gift boxes in different sizes. Some of my students have covered them in pretty paper so that they have something nice to look at each time they open the drawer.

We've saved the most fun for last—closet shelves and floor! If the shelves in your closet are too high for you to reach, make sure that you don't put anything up there that you have to reach very often. Shelves are a good place for out of season purses and shoes, books (certainly not this one), extra boxes and various uncompleted projects. Clear, plastic shoe boxes, or regular boxes well-labeled on the end are super for closet-top spruce up.

Do you throw shoes, dirty clothes, and assorted other goodies in the bottom of your closet at night? Shame on you if you do, since you'll just make life so much harder if you ever need to find anything, and of course, *some day* you will. The plastic, see-through boxes are great here, too, as are any types of boxes, crates, and especially, stacking vegetable bins in pretty plastics. This is a terrific rainy day project, and to do it properly, it will take just about all day.

One of the hardest parts of cleaning out closets and dresser drawers is gaining the ability to get rid of things we no longer need or have use for. Do you still have your very first Halloween costume hanging in your closet? How about the orange lace dress Aunt Lilly gave you two Christmases ago? Get the picture? We have all had things we kept for sentimental (or family) reasons. That's fine. It's important to hold on to special things that have special meaning for us, but those items don't need to take up valuable space in what may be an already crowded closet or drawer.

Keep those treasured items in a chest or trunk for safekeeping. (Close enough, of course, so that you can pull out the orange dress if Aunt Lilly should visit!)

Do you have a hamper for your dirty clothes? If so, please see to it that they make it to the hamper and not under your bed or in the closet. Ask Mother where she would like you to put clothing that is in need of repair. You may be able to sew on a missing button, but you'll probably want her to handle any major repair.

You see, having a place for everything and everything in its place will make you feel so good!

By starting out with an organized, pretty area for your clothes to "live," you'll find that it's so much easier to (1) put together lots of great outfits because you'll spot your garments at a moment's glance, and (2) keep what you have neater and in better shape.

Mom will be tickled pink, and you just may never have to miss the bus again!

Who Are You? Now that you're organized, you'll be able to see at a moment's glance what kind of person you are. Huh? Do you see ten dresses in a row and one pair of pants—or just the opposite?

Have you ever walked into a store, seen an outfit on a mannequin and promptly announced, "Wow, that outfit looks just like Suzie!" Actually, you've just paid Suzie a pretty big compliment because your comment says that Suzie has her own "look." The clothes you wear are your very special way to tell others how you see yourself.

Which look do you have?

1. **Pixie**—Small-boned, petite and has a saucy sort of look. Her hair is usually short and layered (like a pixie) for a youthful, fun look. She wears simple things in bright colors well. Teens with a pixie look wear very natural make-up.

2. **Rustic**—Loves casual clothes like pants and sweaters in earthy, warm colors. If she's a teen, she wears very little make-up. Hair is simple and usually longish.

3. **City Girl**—She has loads of self-confidence and will wear the kookiest, newest thing without a second thought. The bolder, the better with color and style, yet she keeps it simple and uncluttered. Hair will probably be simple to avoid taking away from the sophisticated look.

4. **Jazzy**—Similar to City Girl but would rather be trendy than just confident. Whatever the newest thing is, she will wear it. She's brave enough to wear something new for the very first time. Whatever's the latest, she will love it. Usually prefers pants.

5. **Romantic**—She prefers pearls to plastic bangles, satin instead of denim, and always comes across as feminine. Her hair is usually long and may be softly curled. She may like ruffles and lace, but never overdoes it. She can wear pants and be "all girl."

Did you find yourself in there? What? You said there were a couple of those that sounded like you? Guess what?! You're normal. Most of us have two different fashion personalities—one for dress-up times and another for casual times. Some girls even enjoy the variety of trying out a little of each depending on where they are and what they're doing—which brings me to our next subject.

The Life You Lead and The Clothes You'll Need. Now that you know your fashion personality, can you list some of the factors that influence what you wear? Close your eyes and see how many things you can think of, then check the list below to see how well you did.

1. The dress code at school.
2. How much does it cost?
3. Does it match other garments you already have?
4. What kind of climate do you live in?
5. What do most of your friends wear?
6. Are you athletic or ultra feminine?
7. What do you need clothes for the most?
8. The size and type of community in which you live.
9. Your coloring.
10. Your size and shape.

Did you have some of the same answers as me?

The clothing you will buy and wear will probably be in the following categories:

Day time clothes—for school or (someday) work
Select:
1. Mix and match coordinates
2. Easy fitting knits
3. Easy care clothing
4. Wash-and-wear fabrics.

Play clothes—after school and work, picnics and beach— any outdoor activity—or inside fun!
Select:
1. Wash and wear cottons
2. T-shirt knits
3. Look for comfort.

Something special—church, special luncheon dates, art galleries and museums, etc.
Select:
1. Skirts and soft blouses
2. Nice dresses
3. Dressy pants with pretty sweaters.

Fit for a princess—recitals, pageants, weddings, banquets, or special parties.
Select:
1. Old fashioned, Victorian look
2. Something swirling and feminine
3. Whatever makes you feel extra special.

    Some Helpful Advice on Fabrics. Manmade (synthetic) fabrics certainly have become part of our lives. It's hard to imagine what it was like without rayon, nylon, dacron and orlon—to name a few "ons." However, I'm sure you've noticed that natural fabrics are once again "the thing," and people everywhere are rediscovering just how comfortable, absorbent, and warm natural fabrics really are.

The *synthetic* fibers:

Dacron—A very strong yarn that is used with cotton and wool to help them hold their shape.

Orlon—Found in sweaters and coats, it creates bulk and keeps you warm.

Nylon—Made from coal, air, and water! The fiber is soft to the touch but very tough. Nylon is used to make stockings and hosiery, underwear, blouses, and sleepwear, to name a few.

Acetate—This shiny fiber is made from wood pulp and is usually made into fabrics that are not very expensive. It's used a lot in scarves and blouses. It wrinkles easily.

The *natural* fibers:

Linen—Used in spring and summer, has a look of crispness (but tends to wrinkle); otherwise easy care.

Cotton—Very durable and absorbent, dyes well, provides warmth without weight when layered, not harmed by heat. Aids in moisture evaporation to keep skin cool in summer.

Silk—Woven from the threads produced by the silkworm. Lustrous finish, should not be put in water since it will go limp. Please have dry-cleaned. Can be dyed into beautiful colors.

Wool—Long lasting, strong fiber, spun into wool from sheep's "hair." It is absorbent, resilient (sort of stretchy, and can get pulled out of shape, too). There are a few more animal fibers besides sheep's wool that you may wear: cashmere, alpaca, mohair, and camel hair.

For easy care, wash-and-wear items, polyester blends can be useful. Polyester by itself can be very hot and may not be a good choice in summer. Inexpensive polyester can take on a shiny, almost plastic look that is not very appealing and can make you look dated.

The "naturals" allow your skin to breathe which is much healthier anyway. The key to warmth is in the layering as much as the fabric worn.

Before we get into more of *what to wear* let's talk about
how to *take care* of what we have.

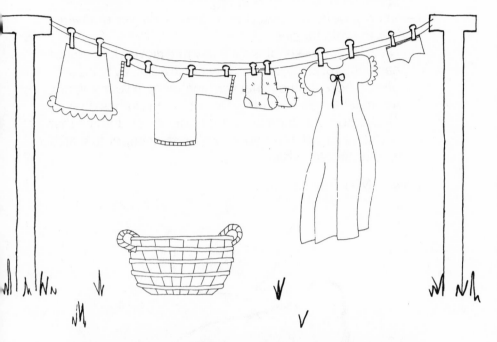

— When you buy a new garment, be certain to keep any tags
  attached that include laundering instructions that may
  not be on the sewn in tags.
— Learn the proper way to help with the laundry; separate
  colors, don't overload the washer, use correct water
  temperature, use bleach only with permission. Use fabric
  softeners to cut down on wrinkles, and never over dry
  your clothes.
— Hang garments up to dry on *plastic* hangers only when still
  slightly damp; you may not need to iron. (Hurray!) If
  ironing is needed, get permission or have Mother do it for
  you.
— If a garment is soiled or damaged, get it taken care of
  before you forget. Never put something away that
  requires attention.
— Never fold or put something away that is too damp since
  it will mildew and acquire a musty odor.

— Don't put shoes in your closet until they have aired out for eight hours, and never, if they have mud or dirt on them. Shoes require weekly cleaning.
— Keep jewelry separated in a dresser drawer or jewelry box to avoid tangles.
— Launder fine washables such as white gloves, lace edged hankies, stockings, and underwear in a sink by hand or in one of those fabulous net washing sacks in your washing machine on gentle setting. Do not put in clothes dryer.
— Please do not establish a daily floor pile of clothing that you've taken off. Have your own pretty hamper to match your bedroom or bath.

How to NOT Buy Lemons!

Don't buy that awesome plaid coat! It looks great, but it's not for each and every occasion.

Do buy a simple, solid style that can be worn everywhere and looks great over everything. Then, by saving money, perhaps you can add the fun coat later.

Don't wear large accessories if you are petite.

Do wear everything in proportion to your body size.

Don't allow undergarments to peek out.

Do wear slips one inch shorter than skirts and dresses, and be certain that no straps of any kind are visible under tank tops or blouses.

Don't wear what everyone else is wearing, if it doesn't look right on you.

Do be an individual and wear only what fits properly.

Don't be a slave to fashion trends by wearing something you feel silly in just to be included or look cool.

Do establish your own fashion statement by experimenting when you shop. Try on lots of different styles until you find the ones that are "you."

Don't wear horizontal (across) stripes on parts of your figure that may be too wide. They will work like an optical illusion and make you look huge!

Don't wear bulky turtleneck sweaters if you have a short neck or a chubby chin.

Do wear simple lines, solid colors, and gentle draping of fabric to hide figure flaws.

Don't buy something that doesn't fit properly, no matter *how* much you love it.

Do hold out for perfection and don't let that money burn a hole in your pocket. (You would *never* do that, now would you?!)

Don't be a prima donna when an adult takes you clothes shopping. The key word is *compromise*.

If you have a problem, **do** be willing to try on selections that you think you may not like—you might be pleasantly surprised. Pretty girls simply shouldn't pout or make a scene in a store (or anywhere).

Don't paw through the merchandise on the racks when shopping, and refrain from showing up with the entire gang from school. Sales people don't like it when everyone crowds into the fitting room at once.

Do explain to the sales person that your mother will be there soon and that you would like to browse around while you are waiting. You are a customer and should not be treated rudely just because you are young. If you get a sales person who is unpleasant or impatient with you, leave and come back with an adult. It would serve no real purpose to argue with the person yourself. Just remember to be polite and pleasant— never silly, giggly, or rude. Two wrongs never make a right, you know!

Don't leave clothing lying on the fitting room floor. Always put it back on the very same hanger—buttons buttoned, zippers zipped, and all fasteners fastened!

Do bring merchandise out of the fitting room in perfect condition.

Don't buy clothing without trying it on first. You are still growing by leaps and bounds, and what fit properly last month may be way too short by now. You never know, and it sure is better to be a smart shopper than to deal with the hassles of returning merchandise.

Do look at yourself in the mirror at all angles before being satisfied enough to own something. Lean over, reach up and bend sideways to make sure the garment is comfortable, not too tight or too short.

Happy Shopping!

Poise

Your Body Speaks Beautifully. What does it mean to you when I say, "Susie is poised?"

Do you get a mental picture of someone who is self-confident, has good posture, doesn't make jerky or nervous movements? You should, because *poise* is the special language that our body silently speaks to others. If I am standing with my arms folded across my chest and tapping my foot, do I look happy and carefree? No, I look impatient. You instantly know what's on my mind. Do your parents have a special body language that tells what their mood is? I'll bet they do. You probably know what they're upset about before they say one word!

Your mannerisms, walk, gestures, and just about everything else you do with your body will be an indication of how much poise or self-confidence you have.

There may be times when you feel that you are "all arms and legs." This is perfectly normal because until you are fifteen or sixteen years old, various parts of the body grow at different rates at different times.

These changes can make a girl feel awkward and ugly, but actually, you're growing prettier. Just remember that most things that are really worth having don't appear overnight, but are nurtured and gently cared for with understanding and patience. Your body is no different.

Poise is simply that special way you carry yourself. It's the difference between dragging your feet and shuffling over to sit in a chair, and holding your head high while you ease effortlessly toward your destination.

It is the efficient use of your body's movement. Once you are able to move about gracefully, being poised will simply be second nature to you. You'll find that you won't even have to concentrate on how to do these things. Then you'll be free to devote all of your attention to more important things—like making new friends and learning new and wonderful things in the world around you!

The proper beginning for doing everything with poise is having good posture. When you stand up straight and tall, you have good posture, and your body will be properly aligned—or stacked up.

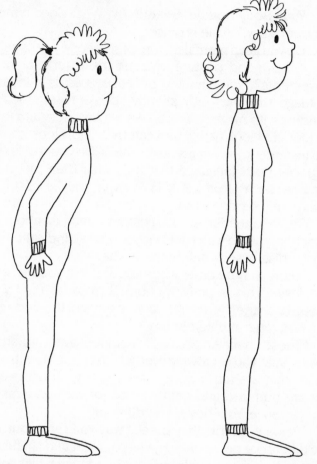

1. Your chin will be parallel with the floor (not pointing up or down).
2. Your earlobes will be placed directly over your shoulders.
3. Your shoulders will be held back, but not rigid.
4. Your tummy will be tucked in, even if you don't have one!
5. Your bottom will be tucked under (no sway-backs, please).
6. Your arms should be relaxed at your side.
7. Your knees should be straight but not locked.
8. Last, but *super* important, is what we do with our feet. It's called a *basic stance*.

The *basic stance* looks a little like the letter "T;" therefore, some people call it a "basic T" or a "model's T."

That's what it *looks* like, but what it *does* is give you a nifty little way to stand so that you'll always look calm, cool, and collected! That could really come in handy during a book report or presentation, don't you think?

A basic stance also looks a little like two o'clock on the face of a clock. The left foot would be the hour hand pointing straight up at the twelve and the right foot would be the minute hand directed at the two.

The left foot is the "front" foot and the right foot is the "back" foot. Be certain to settle the weight of your body onto your back foot so that you won't be leaning forward. When you walk out of a basic stance, you would always use the front foot. Why? That's right. If you try to walk on the back foot, you'll trip a little because you'll need to shift your weight again. It's easy—front foot first—the foot that's all set to go and pointing straight ahead.

I'll bet you never thought that anyone would make up rules for learning how to walk. You learned how to do it when you were just a baby, didn't you? Well, just think of this as the new-and-improved method! Everything you will learn in this book, although some of it may be a little different from what you've done before, is meant to make your life easier and happier.

Now that you're standing properly, let's do a few exercises to be certain that your posture remains picture perfect.

Stand up against a straight wall with the heel of your back foot against the wall. Take your hand and see if it will fit between the wall and your waistline. Is there a big gap? Your hand should just barely fit without lots of extra space. If there is a lot of room left, bend your knees and slowly begin to dip down, keeping your hand behind your back. About half way down, you'll notice that the space between you and the wall has disappeared. Of course, you can't walk away from the wall in a squatting position just to have a straight back, but it really is a great way to remind yourself of what good posture should feel like.

The same exercise can be done lying on a flat surface but instead of gliding down the wall, you simply draw your knees up toward your hips, keeping your feet flat on the floor.

When I first began these exercises, I think you could have driven a truck under my back, but after several weeks of practice, practice, practice, I could just barely wedge my hand in—and the results are beautiful when you proudly walk away.

Have a Seat, Please. You're going to look super while you're standing, but eventually you'll need to pull up a chair—or actually walk over to one. Stand so that your feet are in the basic stance with your back leg touching the front of the chair. Now, place your hands on the front of your thighs to help you keep your balance. Bend your knees, and with your back perfectly straight, lower yourself onto the edge of the chair but don't "melt" into it. If your feet still reach the floor, either keep them in the basic stance or cross your ankles. Fold your hands gracefully and put them in your lap, resting on your left leg (never wedged between your legs, as your knees will push apart! Horrors!).

To stand up, simply reverse the steps, keeping your back straight and your head held high.

These sitting and standing hints will really come in handy the next time you are any place where the eyes are on you!

Floating Through Air. Now that you're almost finished reading this chapter, you can use this book for something else for a while. Have you ever heard of anyone walking with a book on her head? Don't laugh—it's really lots of fun. Place your book on top of your head and don't let go until it feels secure. Now, place your hands down at your side and walk out of your basic stance with your front foot slowly and carefully. We're not running a race—just practicing the regal walk of a princess.

This procedure—although it may make you feel a little self-conscious—is the tried and true method for teaching young girls (and fashion models) the prettiest way to get from one point to another.

Please practice with shoes on, not sneakers, but a shoe with a smooth bottom. It's easier to walk on wood, tile, or linoleum. Carpet makes your feet a little sluggish.

Okay, you're walking along and need to turn and go in the opposite direction. What do you do? A *pivot.*

Pivoting simply means turning around, and yes, you've probably been doing it for years without knowing it.

1. Stand with feet in basic stance position. The front foot is pointed straight ahead toward your audience.
2. Pick up your front foot as if you were going to take a step. Bring your back foot up now, and turn on the balls of your feet. If your *left* foot was your first foot, pivot to the *right.* If it's the *right* foot, pivot to the left. There! You did it!

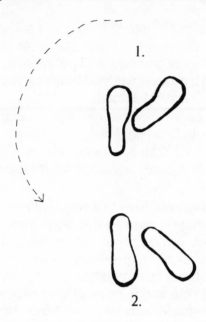

1.

2.

A Few More Poise Pointers.

— If you must open a door to exit one room and enter another, be certain to turn around and face in the direction of the group you are leaving, smile, and acknowledge them as you shut the door in front of you.

— Never straddle a beach towel as you prepare to lower yourself onto the sandy beach since you will form a very alarming view of yourself from the rear! Simply kneel down next to the towel, lower yourself onto your side, and then get situated. Much prettier!

— When picking objects off the floor, always bend from your knees—never lean straight over. This is not attractive and certainly not very good for your back.

— Never crawl into the seat of a car, but lower yourself onto the edge of the seat and swing your legs up and over into the car, keeping your knees together at all times. (Teeny-tiny cars and huge trucks take a little practice—but why would you be getting into a huge truck anyway?!)

Just remember—everything you do is part of the puzzle—the puzzle of helping you to be the very prettiest, the very best *you* that you can be.

What I improved during this chapter:

1. _poise_
2. _hair_
3. _face_
4. _skin_
5. _makeup_

Any more?
Congratulations! You should be very proud of yourself!

Chapter III
Table Etiquette

I have taught many boys and girls and spoken with many parents over the years, and the topic that always comes out tops on the list of priorities is table manners.

When you're just a baby, you have a good excuse for not having proper table skills. But now you are a lady; and a lady will be going to lovely restaurants, dining with friends, adults, and even boyfriends. Imagine how embarrassed you'd be if your peas slid off your fork or your sliced tomato shot across the table! These horrible things will probably never happen to you, but let's just make sure that you're prepared to handle whatever situation comes your way.

As I've mentioned before, most of your moms and dads probably work outside your home. Some of you may be lucky enough to enjoy meals at the dinner table as a family each day, but maybe not. In fact, in most of my classes, the students indicate that at least half of them don't have that opportunity as much as they would like. Why? Different people with different schedules, coming and going, rushing around grabbing a cookie here, a snack there, a fast food burger in between. What it all boils down to is that not all kids get a chance to form good table manner skills at an early age. It doesn't mean that their parents don't care or that they don't care—it simply means that we live in times when life can be hectic. For example, your mom may get off work at five o'clock, your brother might need to be at soccer practice at five forty-five and you might have a ballet class at six fifteen. Meanwhile, Dad picked your sister up from day care and they're both at home starving! Realistically, I can tell you what happens in a lot of families—Dad feeds "Sis" and himself, Mom arrives home an hour later after you and your brother have convinced her to pull into the neighborhood drive-thru. Sound familiar to anyone? Unfortunately, it probably does. I won't go into the nutritional side of this right now (we have a whole chapter for that). The main thing that is missing is the routine that is necessary to form good table manners at home.

Where the "Tools" Go

What tools? Some call it silverware, some call it flatware, some may call them utensils. Whatever they are called, they are used to get your food from place to place while you're enjoying a meal. Once you become familiar with each piece and what it's used for, the fear and mystique of table etiquette will vanish forever!

How It All Began. But first of all, a little history. Although most families use stainless steel utensils for everyday dining, sterling silver is a traditional luxury that most folks save for Sunday dinner, holidays, or other special occasions. Silver has a long history as one of the earth's most precious metals. Museum pieces date back to 1900 B.C.! Pieces of wrought silver were used and treasured throughout the Greek and Roman civilizations. Silver spoons were used long before knives and forks. In England, a silver spoon was actually mentioned in a will in the year 1259! The earliest English fork was dated 1632.

For hundreds of years, knives were the same daggers used in hunting and for self-defense! During what historians call the Restoration Period in England (1660-1685), silver made into various pieces of tableware became generally popular.

Early American Silver. Silversmiths were among the first settlers, bringing with them their Old World skills and traditions. Soon, they developed a distinctive style of their own with clean, simple lines. In 1768, Paul Revere made the famous Revere bowl for the "Fifteen Sons of Liberty." Ask your mom if she has a Revere bowl or if she can show you a picture. Since silver is so durable, many families still have pieces inherited from their colonial ancestors!

The Difference Between Flatware and Holloware. *Flatware* refers to all knives, forks and spoons, including those used in serving foods. *Holloware* refers to all dishes, bowls, tea sets, trays, salt shakers, candlesticks, pitchers, and other pieces used for table service or decoration.

When you hear the word "sterling," it means that there is a very high standard of purity in the silver. Under United States law, only pieces that contain the proper amount of pure silver can be stamped "sterling."

Place Setting Pieces. Although most ladies like for their silver to match and be of only one pattern or design, it is perfectly acceptable to mix pieces if they are family heirlooms. In fact, it can have a very charming effect. Please do not use your mother's good silver without her permission. It is very expensive. If you are permitted to use it, please do not put it in the dishwasher since it is much too hot and abrasive. Wash it gently by hand in warm, soapy water. Dry it immediately and put it back in Mother's silver drawer or chest.

Most ladies use what is called a five-piece place setting. This includes a place knife, place fork, place spoon, salad fork, and teaspoon.

Eventually, ladies like to add serving pieces to their silver service such as a gravy ladle, pie server, vegetable serving spoon, or a cold meat fork to name a few.

Basic Table Settings. There are many correct ways to set a table. In most cases, all you have to do is think about what you are eating and place the utensils in the order they will be used. The outside pieces are used first, then work in towards your plate. When in doubt, follow the host and hostess and do it the same way they do. That way, if they are wrong, at least everyone will be wrong the same way! Never be tempted to correct someone at the table even if you *know* you're right.

My advice to students is that as long as you don't make your mistake obvious and draw great attention to it, it will probably go unnoticed. There's no reason to be so nervous and self-conscious of whether or not you're using the right fork at the exact right moment that you won't enjoy the fine food and pleasant company.

Breakfast

Breakfast is my favorite meal, and I like it to be cheery and bright. Use a colorful tablecloth or placemats and napkins. Bring out your most colorful dishes. It wakes you up as well as your appetite!

Informal Lunch or Dinner

The spoon and fork resting horizontally above the plate are for dessert. Sometimes, they are brought in later with your selection. There are usually no more than three courses for the luncheon and never any more than four for dinner. You may use a tablecloth or placemats. (Never both!)

Formal Dinner

A full-size tablecloth is traditional for a formal dinner.

Obviously, you are not going to use all of these articles each time you dine. In fact, there are several pieces that you probably won't use for a number of years—the wine glass and the cup and saucer (unless you are having very fancy hot cocoa)! This full, formal table setting is for special occasions, holiday meals or surprising your parents on a special day. (Remember, only with permission or supervision).

Additionally, courses may even be added to this table setting such as soup or seafood cocktail. The seafood cocktail is eaten with the "doll-size," three-pronged fork on your far right. It is called a seafood fork. They are normally very pointed, so please be careful. When you are finished, place the fork on your plate. Do not eat left-over cocktail sauce with your spoon; in fact, don't do *anything* with the leftover sauce.

If soup is being served, it comes before the salad, and the bowl will be placed on top of your dinner plate. The soup spoon will be larger than your teaspoon. Always dip your soup spoon away from you and sip from the edge of the spoon without slurping. Do not be tempted to lift the bowl to get the last drop! Leave your spoon on the side of your dinner plate when finished.

There are basically two ways to eat with a knife and fork: the European method, and the American method. The European method is much easier. Leave your fork in your left hand after cutting your food and feed yourself with your left hand (easy for us lefties)! The American method uses sort of a cross-over motion. Cut your food with your right hand. Put your knife down, switch the fork from your left hand to your right hand. Finally, you get to eat!

Although there is no right or wrong way, you may find after practice that the European method is a little easier.

When you are finished, your knife and fork will go side by side on the top right side of the plate and cross the plate diagonally. The tines (or prongs) of your fork should face down, and your knife blade should extend about one-half inch over the side of the plate.

Using the *finished* position is a lot nicer than pushing yourself away from the table and moaning, "I'm stuffed!"

However, if you just need a minute to let your food settle or to contemplate another buttered roll, use the rest position which is simply forming an "X" in the center of your plate by crossing the downward tines of your fork over the blade of your knife. Again, clear about one-half inch over the edge of your plate.

The Bread & Butter Plate. The small plate in the general area above your forks is for bread, crackers, and butter. There may or may not be a small butter knife placed horizontally across the top portion of the plate. Take bread or rolls as they are passed around the dinner table *one at a time* only, even though you are positive you could eat two. After you finish the first one, decide if you have room! Break off small bite size pieces and butter them only *as you are ready to eat them.* This procedure is done directly over your bread and butter plate. The butter knife stays on the top portion of the plate when not in use. Oh, please remember, don't put a *mountain* of butter on your plate. If the butter is wrapped in foil, place the folded trash on the bread and butter plate.

The Salad Course. Your mom may serve salad in a bowl for you at home because it's easier to eat, but actually, a salad should be served on a salad plate. In nicer restaurants, your salad will be brought to you on a chilled plate immediately after you have finished your soup course (provided you had one). The waiter or waitress will simply switch your soup bowl and soiled spoon for your fresh salad. Look up at your server at this point and say "Thank you." As I mentioned before, it is important to be courteous to the people who serve us and help us in public.

A salad should be in pieces that don't need cutting and can be easily eaten with your salad fork. That doesn't always happen though. I'm the first one to admit that if a slice of tomato would look prettier left uncut on my finished salad, I may be tempted to leave it that way for serving purposes. It is, therefore, acceptable to cut your salad as you enjoy it. Salads are truly one of my favorites. Not only do they look pretty, they're so nutritious!

The Dessert Course. Ever since I was a little girl, I have remembered how to spell *dessert* by knowing that since lots of people would like to eat *doubles*, there are double S's in the word! It may sound silly, but it works. Most desserts are very easy to eat because they require only a spoon or fork. Some types of desserts may require that use you both, such as cakes with gooey or runny fillings. Use common sense and do what will be less messy. If the fillings or sauces contain fruits that are too large to be eaten whole, it's alright to cut them first.

The Fingerbowl. Although they are not used very frequently, a fingerbowl serves an important purpose when present. Strong, smelly seafood, or fruit desserts that may stain your fingers or table linens, and other stains can be easily removed with a fingerbowl of cool water with a slice of lemon floating in it. The lemon removes odors, and when rubbed on skin, can sometimes take away stains.

Setting the Mood. I am a true believer in setting the proper atmosphere in which to eat when setting the table. It was my favorite task to help my mom with when I was a little girl, and I have never tired of it. Many times when I have prepared a relatively simple meal, I am praised because the table looks so nice. Having an attractive table helps to make the most ordinary meal special.

Ask Mother's permission to have one opportunity each week to set the table (more if you like). Be creative. Bring some fresh flowers in from the garden, try out one of our nifty napkin tricks, or plan a theme table such as tropical, circus, or an indoor picnic. Use your imagination!

Just for Fun. As I mentioned earlier, my favorite chore to help my mom with was setting the table.

In addition to color coordinating lovely dishes, flatware and glasses, the napkins you use can add fun and flair to an otherwise ordinary table setting. The art of napkin folding will be a great way to impress your friends and family the next time everyone gathers around the table! (It's also a great way to make even beans and franks seem elegant!)

Napkins have been used since the Middle Ages. Before that, people used everything from their shirt sleeves to corners of the tablecloth for wiping their mouths. Napkins are now a regular part of any table setting. Disposable paper napkins are convenient, and most households use them at some point. However, make certain that you have at least one basic set of cloth napkins on hand for special occasions. (This might make a nice gift for your mother sometime.)

Tips:
— Napkins should be *square*.
— Napkins should be starched and ironed (with supervision).
— Experiment with different types; you can even use paper!

Glass Fan

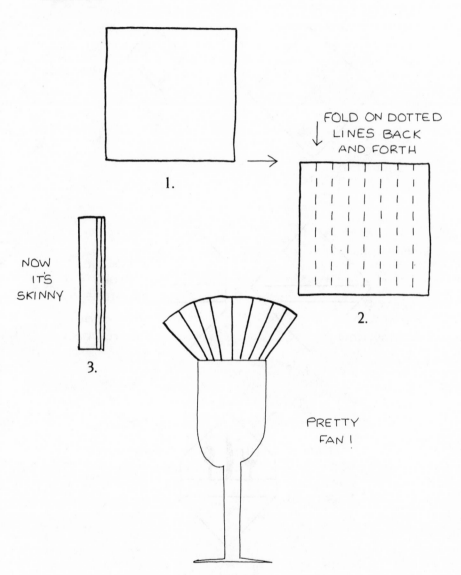

1.

FOLD ON DOTTED
LINES BACK
AND FORTH

2.

NOW
IT'S
SKINNY

3.

PRETTY
FAN !

1. Fold napkin in half.
2. Make one-inch accordion pleats all the way down.
3. Place folded end into a glass and let the other end fan out.

Sleeping Bag

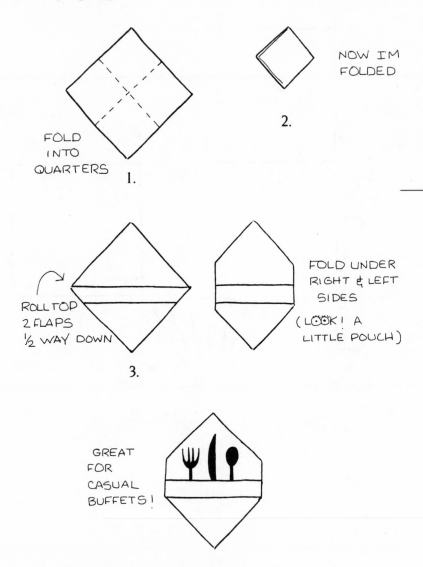

FOLD
INTO
QUARTERS

1.

NOW I'M
FOLDED

2.

ROLL TOP
2 FLAPS
½ WAY DOWN

3.

FOLD UNDER
RIGHT & LEFT
SIDES

(LOOK! A
LITTLE POUCH)

GREAT
FOR
CASUAL
BUFFETS!

1. Fold napkin in half.
2. Take the top flap and fold in half.
3. Flip napkin over and fold into quarters; now insert your
   utensils, serving end up in the little pouch!

The Lily

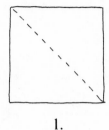

1.

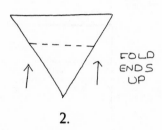

FOLD
ENDS
UP

2.

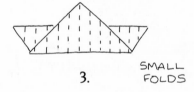

3.

SMALL
FOLDS

4.

1. Fold napkin in half diagonally to form a triangle.
2. Turn up the bottom points on both sides leaving about three inches in the middle.
3. Fold in one-inch accordion pleats (like Glass Fan).
4. Place the bottom in a shallow glass or in a napkin ring; fan the top out to look like a flower.

The Bandit—for soft drink bottles; great for cook-outs

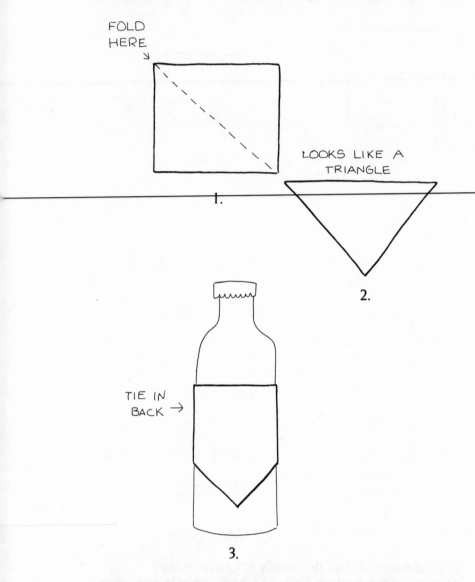

FOLD
HERE

LOOKS LIKE A
TRIANGLE

1.

2.

TIE IN
BACK →

3.

1. Fold napkin (or bandana) diagonally to form a triangle.
2. Tie around middle of bottle, secure ends in a knot.
   These are just a few; you'll probably make up others as you experiment.

Dictionary of Possible Dining Disasters for Dimpled Darlings
or
Difficult Foods and Embarrassing Situations

It's wise to occasionally prepare for disasters—just in case they occur. (You do know, of course, that if you prepare for them, they will never materialize.) Let's discuss some in alphabetical order:

Allergies—Your hostess has just served strawberries and creme for dessert, and they make you break out in three-quarter-inch hives. Don't embarrass your hostess by shrieking at the very sight of the dish nor do you want to bore everyone with a lengthy talk about your allergies and other health problems. Simply say, "No, thank you. I don't care for any."

Apples—Apples are not difficult to eat if you're at a picnic. Just pick up a juicy, shiny one and enjoy. However, if you're at the table, please cut in quarters and eat with a knife and fork.

Artichokes—They are an exciting and nutritious finger food. The leaves are pulled off one at a time. Hold leaf by pointed end and dip lighter colored meaty end into the sauce if there is one provided. (It will probably be a lemony, butter and egg sauce called "hollandaise.") With or without sauce, pull the leaf through your front teeth to remove the soft meaty part. Keep the used leaves neatly on your plate as you finish. The treasure is the cone shaped heart of the artichoke that you will find after finishing all the leaves. You'll come to a fuzzy part called the "choke." Do not eat this part, but cut and eat the heart. It's a delicacy! (Hint: Have Mother buy an artichoke for you to practice with at home first.)

Asparagus—If it's cooked, there's no question that you must eat this vegetable with your fork. If it's fresh or lightly steamed, you may eat it with your fingers if it is being served as an appetizer or hors d'oeuvre. Closer to the tip, the parts will be more tender and easier to eat. Use a cocktail plate or napkin as a helper.

Avocados—When they are served cut in half with the dark bumpy skin still attached, scoop out and eat with a spoon. If the hollow in the center is filled with salad, eat with your fork. Avocados are very good snacks.

Baked Potatoes—Remove and discard foil wrapping if present by rolling into a small ball and placing under edge of bread plate. Season your potato, and eat it with your fork. Cut the skin with your knife and fork. It's full of vitamins and minerals and is a special treat not to be neglected.

Bananas—One of nature's easier foods; it even comes with its own hand-protecting wrapper. However, bananas are only eaten monkey style in a casual setting. If you're ever served one at the dinner table, peel it all the way on a plate, put the skin on the side and cut into bite size pieces. Ever notice how we all tend to put too much banana in our mouths and end up looking like chipmunks! Well, no more.

Berries—Eat with your spoon as opposed to chasing the rolypolies around your plate or bowl with a fork. If you are served whole, fresh strawberries with a dip, pick the berry up by the stem, dip it lightly and bite, taking care not to drip juice on you or on the table linen.

Blowing Your Nose—It's disgusting just thinking about it, but sometimes it just can't be helped. It should, however, be avoided at the table. Excuse yourself to the ladies room. (See sneezing.)

Bread and Rolls—Break off small bite-sized portions individually, buttering them as you eat them. Remember, never spread butter on them like you were icing a cake. Always do this over a plate.

Burping—Another necessary bodily function that should never be performed deliberately. If it happens, keep your mouth closed (muffles the sound), and say,"Excuse me." Absolutely never laugh or giggle if someone at the table burps on purpose. You will only add fuel to the fire and encourage that poor soul to do something even worse. In some countries, burping after a meal is considered a compliment to the cook. If you're reading this book, you probably don't live in one of those countries.

Cake—If it is a dry, firm cake such as pound cake that doesn't have frosting or filling, it's alright to hold it on a napkin and break off bite size pieces with your fingers. Otherwise, use a fork. I've been to several wedding receptions where cake with lots of frosting flowers was served on napkins without forks. Resist the temptation to take the piece with the most icing or you are in for a messy challenge.

Candy—"Oh brother!" you're probably thinking; "a rule for eating *candy!*" This applies to the fancy type that comes nestled in its own little paper nest. You are to take the first, and only, one you touch when the box or plate is passed to you. Pick it up, paper and all, and eat with fingers. (Please resist the urge to pinch out pieces to see what the filling is!)

Chicken—This doesn't have anything to do with the apprehension you might feel for all of these new table manners to learn! Actually, this delicious, all-American treat should be eaten with the help of a knife and fork unless it is crisply fried and eaten at a picnic.

Choking—Certainly no laughing matter. The international sign for choking is to grasp your neck and reach out for help with the other. I would imagine this action would be automatic if you were really choking. A person in trouble would not be able to cough or talk. Immediately, someone should be summoned who knows the Heimlich Maneuver.

Clams—If you live by the seashore and have an opportunity to try clams or other shellfish, you're in for a treat. When clams are steamed, the shell will open up part of the way, and you can use your fingers or your fork to carefully open it enough to reach in with your fork and lift out the clam. Either dip it in melted butter or cocktail sauce, or enjoy the delicious taste alone (all done over a plate, of course).

Corn on the Cob—Butter and season lightly to avoid a drippy mess. Grasp each end securely, either with your fingers or by using the stick-in type holders if they are provided. Do not chomp noisily like a piglet on a farm or chew back and forth like a typewriter carriage!

Coughing—Turn away from the table, and please cover your mouth with your napkin. A sip of your beverage may soothe your throat. You may need to be excused for a minute if your coughing spell persists.

Dip—In the event that raw vegetables are served with dip, please place a spoonful of dip on your plate along with the vegetables. Do not hang over the veggie tray and crunch cauliflower! The same applies to chips, etc.

Fishbones—Tiny terrors! Beware, since they can sneak up on you quickly. Carefully remove with with your fingers and place on edge of your plate.

Fly in Soup, etc.—It rarely happens, but it is a possibility. If it occurs in a restaurant, quietly get your waiter's attention. Do not jump up and down screaming, "Bug! Bug! Help!" That's not really fair. I'm sure you will cheerfully be presented with a replacement and many apologies. If you're a dinner guest in a home and discover an unwelcome guest, don't do *anything* except move to the next course. If a fly drops by and decides to take a dip in your lemonade, that's a different story—ask for another.

Fruit Cocktail—Use a spoon; don't stab the pieces of fruit individually.

Grapefruit Half—There are special grapefruit spoons with peaked tips that will easily dislodge a grapefruit section from its rind, but if one is not available, use a dessert spoon, being careful to not squirt juice when you dig in. After eating the fruit, you may use your spoon to drink any leftover juice as you would soup. P*lease* do not pick up the rind and squeeze it into your spoon, not even in private because you may forget and do it in front of the cutest boy in school someday!

Grapes—The seedless ones are easy. Break a small section of stems off of the whole bunch. Eat them *one at a time*, putting the whole grape in your mouth. If you're eating the seeded variety, take the seeds out of your mouth by removing them into a paper napkin after you have chewed and swallowed the fruit.

Gravy—Use the gravy ladle or spoon to apply gravy to food; don't pour it on like a pitcher. Less is better; more is messy.

Gristle—This is the chewy, fatty substance often found in meats. If gristle finds its way into your mouth, carefully and discreetly expel it into your napkin (paper, if possible) and put it under the rim of your plate. Do not attempt to swallow it. The waiter can bring you another napkin if you are at a restaurant.

Hiccups—Again, if your mouth is closed, the sound will be muffled. Some widely used remedies include drinking water, eating honey, holding your breath, and having someone frighten you (my least favorite). If you are at the table and they become annoying, excuse yourself until they have settled down.

Lobster—A real food challenge but well worth it. If you can master the art of lobster eating, please put a gold star right here on this page. Your "equipment" should consist of a nutcracker, a pick, a seafood fork, a fingerbowl, plenty of napkins, and a bib. Yes, a bib. My first real experience was in Newport, Rhode Island one summer on vacation. My family and I found a real seafood restaurant with real lobster, and the waitress brought us three bibs, and only one of us was seated in a high-chair! Right away I knew this would be a challenge. A lobster revolts at being your dinner right from the very beginning. He will sometimes spray water when cracked open. Carefully twist off large claws with your hands. Crack the claws with the nutcracker and pull the meat out with your pick. The larger pieces of meat in the body and tail are much easier to remove and should be eaten with a knife and fork. If a sauce is offered, use your fork for dipping. The greenish color in the lobster's middle is called *tamale* (liver), and the pinky-coral color is the roe. Both are considered real delicacies and should at least be tried. Please ask an adult for help when using the nutcracker and pick. Enjoy!

Melon—Small cubes or balls may be eaten with your spoon. Watermelon is eaten with a fork, avoiding seeds with each fork full. If you do get one, swallow the fruit; then, discreetly expel the seed onto the fork and then place on edge of plate. If the watermelon is offered at a picnic, it is absolutely all-American to eat by holding wedges in your hand. However, a lady never engages in seed spitting contests!

Nachos—Eat as you would dips and crunchies.

Pasta (or spaghetti)—Back in the "olden days" when there was only one shape of spaghetti noodle, there was only one acceptable way to eat it—wind it around your fork at a slant using your spoon as a prop, then bring a realistic amount up to your mouth using only the fork. Do not suck a wayward noodle back into your mouth with a loud slurp; gently help it with your fork. Spaghetti is not cut up unless for a small child. There are many spoon and fork sized pastas popular now that are delicious and easy to eat.

Shish Kebob—Carefully hold the end of the skewer with one hand and gently guide the food off with your fork with the other hand. Skewer should be placed on edge of plate. Cut and eat each piece as usual.

Shrimp—Small shrimp in a cocktail sauce are eaten whole with your seafood fork. Sitting around peeling and eating steamed shrimp with family and friends is a wonderful pastime as well as a delicious treat that may be enjoyed with your fingers. A fingerbowl with lemon would be nice.

Sneezing—This is certainly a normal body function, and if you're like most of us, a sneeze will come on pretty suddenly. Simply turn away from your neighbors, and cover your mouth and nose with your napkin. Gesundheit!

Soup—Don't put too much in your soup spoon and make sure you work the spoon away from you and then up to your mouth. Never slurp and never blow on hot soup. Let it cool naturally. Please do not tilt the bowl to retrieve the last spoonful and never pick the bowl up and drink (exception: small oriental broth cups).

Tea Bag—When drinking hot tea, remove bag with spoon, gently pressing it against inside of cup before removing. Place tea bag on saucer next to cup.

Whole Fish—It is rare that a restaurant would serve a young person a whole fish (that includes the head). However, anything's possible, so let's learn how to eat one. After the head has been removed, make a long slit from end to end with your knife, lay the fish open with your fork, place the tip of your knife under the backbone, lift it out whole. As you eat, refer to *Fishbones* in this section.

When in Doubt

Finger Foods

Pizza slice
Corn on the cob
Raw asparagus
Artichoke
Steamed shrimp
Hot dog in bun
Hamburger in bun
Pickles
Spare ribs
Onion rings
French fries (unless globbed with ketsup)

Fork Foods

Asparagus in sauce
Baked potato
Shrimp in sauce
Pork chops
Open-faced sandwiches
Cherry tomatoes
Pie
Sticky cake
Meats in a sauce
Fried chicken (except at picnics)
Melon (except watermelon at a picnic)

Understanding Menus

The following terms are used in restaurants and in the menus you may be given to choose your meal from:

A *la*—a French term meaning "in the style of."

A *la carte*—dishes that have to be individually ordered, as distinct from a complete meal that usually includes an appetizer, salad, main course, and dessert for one price.

A *la king*—chopped food, usually chicken or turkey, in a cream sauce with sliced mushrooms and pimento.

A *la maison*—in the style of the restaurant or the house specialty.

A *la mode*—pie or dessert topped with a scoop of ice cream.

Amandine—made or served with almond nuts.

Au *gratin*—a dish that's browned in the oven or broiler, usually topped with buttered bread crumbs or grated cheese, or both.

Au jus—food, usually roast beef, served in its own juices.

Butterfly—to split food down the center but not quite all the way through so that the two halves can be opened flat like butterfly wings; often done with large shrimp or a thick fillet of steak when ordered well done.

Cafe au lait—coffee with cream or milk.

Canape—small toast pieces covered with food spread.

Carte du jour—menu of the day.

Cordon Bleu—filled with cheese, ham, or Canadian bacon.

Crepe—thin French pancake.

Du jour—it means "of the day," like "soup de jour."

En brochette—food that is cooked on a skewer.

En concatte—cooked in a casserole.

Flambe—desserts soaked in liquor and set ablaze; you should never do this without a grown-up present.

Fricassee—this describes chicken or small game that's cooked in a sauce, usually with vegetables, after first being cut up and browned.

Fromage—French word for cheese.

Hors d'oeuvres—foods served as appetizers.

Julienne—cut in thin strips.

Marinate—to steep (soak) meat, fish, fowl, vegetables, or other food in a spicy or sweet liquid for several hours until the food absorbs the flavor.

Poisson—French word for fish.

Poulet—French word for chicken.

Provencale—dishes that are served with garlic, onion, mushrooms, herbs, and olive oil.

Puree—to grind to paste either by pressing through a food mill or whirling in an electric blender.

Ragout—a hearty brown stew, highly seasoned.

Sauteed—fried in a small amount of hot oil or butter.

Souffle—very light egg mixture, whipped until it's frothy, then baked until puffy.

Table d' hote—one price for the entire meal.

Veau—French word for veal.

Viande—French word for meat.

Volaille—French word for poultry.

After reading these, the menu still may seem "Greek" to you. Most of these terms are from the French language. Menu terms in an Italian restaurant will probably be in Italian. Some menus list English translations on the side. If not, ask an adult at the table to interpret or to ask the waiter to do so. When you are older and are dining with friends and no adult is present, simply smile and ask the waiter or waitress to translate! If understanding is not the problem, but pronouncing it is, simply lift your menu when the waiter or waitress comes around, point to the mystery dish of your choice, and hope for the best! Ask for pronunciation for future reference.

Restaurants

Going to a restaurant is a special occasion. For most young people, it doesn't really matter whether it's the neighborhood hamburger hang-out or the fanciest place in town. It's just exciting to go someplace different to eat once in a while. Have you ever noticed how everything seems to taste and look better than it does at home? Moms find this unusual fact most distressing!

Although most of the rules in the table etiquette chapter are for "nicer" restaurants, you will want to take the basic knowledge you are gaining here and use it everywhere. You know something? If you always use "special place" manners and etiquette, you won't ever slip up and forget to use them when you *really* have to—you'll simply do it as second nature.

The great thing about dining out with adults is that all you have to do is basically decide what you want, convey the information to them, and they will handle it. The same thing goes if you need more milk, dropped your fork (never pick it up; leave it on the floor, it will be cleared by the bus person), or need other assistance.

However, when you are old enough (and many of you are) to eat in a restaurant with your friends, you have every right to ask questions about the things you do not understand. In some restaurants, there are daily specials not included on the printed menu. I've been to restaurants where the waiters describe these specials using more exciting adjectives than your English teacher knows. These flowery terms often include everything but the price! Don't be embarrassed to ask. Better that you know *before* you and your friends end up with a part-time job washing dishes there! Seriously, at your age, I doubt that any reputable restaurant would describe such specials and not offer you price information.

If you are dining by yourself, or with friends, make sure you have enough money before you place your order.

The Who's Who of Restaurants. You may already be familiar with some of the people and what they do, but here's a short review in the order that you will encounter them:

Maitre d'—(pronounced may-treh-dee) He is the head waiter. The fancier the restaurant, the more elegantly he will be dressed—a tuxedo perhaps. He's in charge of the other waiters, and it is also his responsibility to see that everyone is seated efficiently. If your family has a certain restaurant that they go to on special occasions, you may see your dad tip the maitre d' from time to time. Perhaps your mom has a favorite table at which to sit, and your dad wants to assure that it has been reserved for you. The maitre d' is usually very charming and friendly. In some restaurants he may also be the manager or owner.

Hostess—If the restaurant is not quite as fancy, there will be a hostess to seat you and your family. She will probably be the one to give you your menus as well. A girl or woman always follows the hostess (or maitre d') to the table and the man follows behind the woman.

Waiter or Waitress—They may wear name tags or introduce themselves to you by their first names. They will take your order and serve your food. Be pleasant and smile. This is not an easy job. Speak clearly and try not to change your mind after placing the order. Should you need the waiter's or waitress' assistance, do not call, "Hey You," or "Boy," but "Waiter," or "Miss" if you cannot remember their name. They receive a tip of 15-20 percent of the entire check total.

Busboy—This person is the waiter's or waitress' assistant. He will clear tables, bring water, and keep your table clean and orderly. Your waiter or waitress will split the tip from the check with him.

Restroom Attendant or Valet—In nicer restaurants, there may be a lady in the restroom to offer you fresh towels, hand lotion, etc. You will normally see restroom attendants in the evening hours. If you are under thirteen, you need not tip the customary twenty-five or fifty cents.

Dining With A Group. Enjoying a meal with a large group of friends is such fun. There are basically two ways of dining with large groups—banquet and buffet style.

In a banquet, you will be served from your left. The waiter or waitress will approach each guest and offer the different courses of your meal. You need only wait for the people at your table to be served, and when the adults begin eating, you may also. You may have lots of opportunities to attend banquets with school or church groups, your parents' jobs, award ceremonies or scout groups. Because of the variety of people you will be with, you'll want to take special pride in your manners and polish up your conversation skills. Don't be nervous, even if you end up seated next to your teacher, troop leader, or coach! Most people look for something to do when they get nervous. Do not start digging into the bread basket and nibbling before the main meal is served.

I firmly believe that young people should be seated with a friend when attending a banquet. Even the most outgoing girl or boy may feel uncomfortable around a number of strangers all at once. Perhaps you could be seated between one new friend and one old one!

A buffet is the same once you're seated, but you'll serve yourself from a long line of tables all stocked with a delicious array of foods. You may find buffet lines at banquets, restaurants, wedding receptions, even fast food salad bars!

Are your eyes bigger than your stomach? My dad used to accuse me of that quite a bit! It means that you put food on your plate as if you had never eaten and halfway through the meal announce, "I'm full!"

It's so tempting to do this in a buffet line because everything looks so delicious. Only take a realistic amount to start with. When you finish, I'm sure you'll be allowed seconds.

Since some buffet lines can be rather long, it is acceptable to begin eating when you return to your place at the table, provided the adults or those in charge have also returned.

If you need replacement silverware or more beverage, simply handle this in the same manner as you would in a restaurant. Remember, always say "please" and "thank you," and a pleasant smile adds just the right touch in any situation.

Do's and Don't's for Dining

We've talked about how to set the mood with an attractive table, the proper restaurant terms, and how to eat just about everything. Now let's discuss a few gentle reminders of what can make or break the mood—at home or at a restaurant.

Do:

— Sit up straight.
— Unfold your napkin (halfway) and place it on your lap as soon as you're seated.
— Wait for the host or hostess to begin eating before you do
— Bow your head quietly when others are saying grace— even if you choose not to participate.
— Ask partners at the table to pass items to you rather than *stretch* your arms across the table.
— Place your napkin in your chair if you need to be temporarily excused.
— Always ask permission to be excused (you *knew* this was coming)!
— Try a new food often.
— Say "please" and "thank you" to those serving you (not just in a restaurant, but *everywhere*).
— Be prompt for mealtime.
— Be neat and clean.

Don't:

— Be frightened by all the rules (remember, *doing* is *understanding*).
— Cough or sneeze without covering your mouth and nose with a handkerchief, tissue, or at least your hand (use your napkin as a last resort).
— Cut up all your food at once (one to three pieces at a time).
— Play with your food.
— Butter a whole roll, biscuit, or piece of bread all at once and eat like a sandwich.
— Ever put a utensil that has already touched your mouth on a serving dish.
— Put your knife in your mouth for any reason.
— Put your elbows on the table (or feet!).
— Wipe your mouth with your napkin as if you were mopping the floor; gently pat your lips.
— Talk with *anything* in your mouth—food, utensil, straw, etc.
— Blow bubbles into straws.
— Play with your hair or comb at the table.

— Leave spoon in coffee cup or small dessert bowl; it may cause a spill.
— Place utensils on table after they have touched food or been in your mouth.

Table Etiquette
True or False

Circle your answers below—No peeking!

1. Your napkin is placed on your seat if you have to be excused temporarily during a meal. **T** F

2. Ask your tablemates to pass items to you instead of stretching and reaching across the table. **T** F

3. It's much better to cut up your steak in bite size pieces before you begin eating; it saves so much time. T **F**

4. Table linen should always be white or ivory. T **F**

5. A loud, satisfied burp following your meal is the ultimate compliment to the chef. T F

6. Unfold and place your napkin on your lap as soon as you are seated. **T** F

7. Never place used silverware directly on the table. **T** F

8. A waiter or waitress serves you from the left. **T** F

9. A hostess always serves herself first. T **F**

10. When serving yourself from a serving dish, always replace the utensils face down and side by side in the dish. **T** F

Answers: 1. T; 2. T; 3. F; 4. F; 5. F; 6. T; 7. T; 8. T; 9. F; 10. T

121

Chapter IV
Health and Fitness

My Body, the Car??

I know what you're probably thinking—"What in the world is this lady talking about? My body looks absolutely *nothing* like my dad's car."

Sure, it doesn't *look* like a car at all—but there are a few similarities that make it easier to remember how to take care of our bodies, on the inside and on the outside.

Let's take a closer look at that amazing piece of machinery we all own—our body.

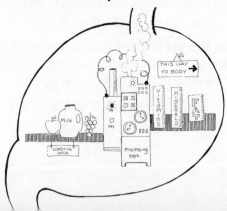

Beauty is an "Inside Job." There are thirty trillion tiny laboratories inside our bodies. Each one is an expert at its own line of work; bone cells, brain cells, skin cells, nail cells, and hair cells. It is really amazing that each one knows exactly what to do and when.

Your body is the most remarkable piece of automatic machinery in the world. It is automatically heated and cooled and has a communication system that makes the most advanced computer seem like a toy! It even has its own delivery and storage system—your **digestive** system. It is able to bring raw materials in and carry waste products away, carry the blood stream throughout your body, sending life and beauty to each of your cells, bones, nerves, muscles, skin, teeth, fingernails, and every hair on your pretty head!

The really amazing part is that your body has the power to turn broccoli, cereal, ham and cheese sandwiches, or milk into the "fuel" needed to "run" your body every day. It works continuously, never taking a break.

The assembly line in your body is called the **alimentary canal**. This hollow tube, running through your body, is more than five times your height! This tube works like an assembly line. The work performed in this assembly line is *not* to put things together, though, but to take them apart. Every bit of food that you eat has to be broken down into different units so that your body can reassemble it into "nutrition."

This assembly line starts to work as soon as you put food in your mouth and begin to chew (and *please*, chew it well). As you chew and chew, the **saliva** in your mouth softens the food and prepares it for its journey. Next step—the stomach, a mixer that grinds and churns the food along with chemicals and **enzymes** like **pepsin** and **rennin** (they are found in our bodies already) that break down the proteins. The stomach is really nothing more than a wide place in the alimentary canal. It can only hold about a quart and a half at a time. The stomach is a pretty busy place, but most of the work is not done there, but in the small intestine.

The small intestine is twenty-one feet long! Well, that is if you stretch it out from end to end which you don't want to do! It stays neatly coiled up inside your body. It is lined with **villi**, small "buds" that stick out and "catch" the food substances that are being broken down. Molecule by molecule, the food substances are absorbed into your blood as they are separated from the rest of the "mixture" sent down from the stomach. There are about five million villi in your small intestine! If you added up how much of an area of food substance these villi could "catch," it would be about the same size as your living room floor!

That's just a small portion of your digestive tract. It's pretty fancy, but nature has taken care of all the instructions on how to make it work. Your job is to make sure that the foods going into the "factory" are pretty ones—not ugly ones.

For more information on your digestive system, look up the words in bold print in your encyclopedia. You just might be surprised at how interesting it is!

By the way, do you know what parts of the "car" we just described?

1. _____

2. _____

You have probably heard people say, "You are what you eat." How true that statement is. What goes in your mouth determines *exactly* what you will look like on the outside. To keep the exterior looking its best, you must really think about what's going in your mouth.

How often do you rush in the door from school starving? Of course, you're not really starving, but you may feel like you are as you run in, open a bag of cookies, and dig in. A few minues later, you're full and happy. But healthy? No!

Okay. Let's be honest. If I run in our house and just *have* to have a snack and I have a choice between a gooey, chocolate doughnut and raw vegetables that still need to be washed and cut, what do you think I'm going to do? Right! Go for the doughnut! That's normal and it's what most of us would do. So, when you're not even hungry, take the time to prepare some healthy snacks that are easy and can be stored for those after school "snack attacks."

Always have an adult's permission before preparing anything in the kitchen. Knives, food processors, and mixers can be dangerous. When using a knife or the stove and oven, also have adult supervision. And. . .ask any mom what one of the most important parts of cooking is—the clean-up.

Happy snacking, girls!

Happy Snacks. . .Healthy Snacks

Frozen Banana Pop
Ingredients: 1 ripe banana
                 2 tablespoons finely chopped nuts
Tools: 1 popsicle stick
                 Wax paper

Spread the nuts on the wax paper. Peel the banana and carefully push the popsicle stick up through the center. Roll the banana around in the nuts so that they stick. Gently wrap in the wax paper and freeze for one hour or more. Serve frozen.

Applesauce Eye Opener
Ingredients: 6 medium-sized apples, unpeeled
                 ½ cup water
                 Honey
                 Cinnamon
                 Raisins
Tools: 1 small paring knife
                 1 saucepan
                 1 spoon

Wash the apples and cut them in quarters, discarding the core. Put them in a saucepan with the water. Put the lid on the pan and cook the apples slowly, stirring occasionally for fifteen minutes. Remove from heat and let them cool for ten minutes. Stir two tablespoons of honey into the warm applesauce. Sprinkle with raisins and cinnamon. Serve warm for breakfast or cold for snack.

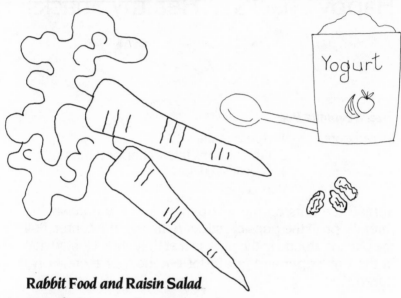

Rabbit Food and Raisin Salad

Ingredients:	2 carrots
	2 apples, unpeeled
	1 celery rib
	½ cup raisins
	1 teaspoon lemon juice
	½ cup plain yogurt
	¼ cup sunflower seeds
Tools:	Vegetable parer
	Wax paper
	Vegetable grater
	Paring knife
	Large bowl
	Measuring cups
	Large wooden spoon

Wash apples and cut in small pieces, discarding core. Wash celery and chop in small pieces. Wash carrots and scrape outside layer with vegetable peeler; throw away peel. Grate carrots onto wax paper. Put apples, celery, carrots and raisins in bowl. Sprinkle with lemon juice. Stir in yogurt and sprinkle with sunflower seeds. Chill and serve. Feeds you and three friends with the munchies!

Mrs. Dyer's Delicious Delight

Ingredients: Milk
1 ripe banana
3 strawberries
Orange juice
Wheat germ
Ice cubes

Tools: Blender
Measuring cup

Fill a blender pitcher one-half full of milk. Add one-half cup of orange juice, one peeled banana broken in small pieces, three strawberries without the stems and three or four small ice cubes. Blend until smooth. Add a sprinkle of wheat germ and blend again. This healthy and *filling* drink is ready to drink now, but if you would like to add a super burst of protein and nutrition, add one raw egg and blend *very* well. Store any leftover in your refrigerator in the pitcher. Blend again before serving. Makes a great breakfast or snack.

The great thing about these snacks is that you can make them at night after you do your homework and store them in your refrigerator so that they'll be ready when you are!

Girls, *please* have your folks read this, too. I spoke with Jan Johnson, vice-president and wellness specialist of The Super Club Kid's Fitness Clubs based in Virginia Beach, Virginia, and she offered this information for parents seeking additional support for children in areas of fitness and nutrition.

"Children tend to listen for advice from an outsider (professional) more seriously than from their parents. Most parents are not very knowledgeable in *specific* areas of fitness and health. They generally recognize the problem, particularly with the overweight child, but generally don't know what to do about it. The same applies to fitness; even if the parent recognizes that their child is out of shape, they do not feel comfortable in setting a program for their child. Even parents that are into fitness activities themselves are not sure how much is too much, etc.

"I feel the extent of professional intervention depends on the family's individual situation. Whether it is spending initial consultation time with a health professional and the parent and child work together, or whether the child is enrolled in a formal program is a decision that each family needs to make. Children will generally be more successful in their goals if they are involved in a group atmosphere with other children. Another positive feature of an organized program/class is from a time discipline perspective. It is difficult for many people to designate a specific time in their personal schedule to discuss diet and fitness goals with their children. It always seems that something else comes up and that meeting is rescheduled.

"Any behavior change requires education. Overweight children and/or unfit children need to understand why it is important for the health of their bodies to be at a desirable percent of body fat and a healthy fitness level. Children need to start taking responsibility for their bodies."

Jan added these following helpful hints for young girls and adolescents:

— Ask the following questions. What type of foods do I eat? Fried foods, foods high in fat, and processed sugar are YUKS! Regular soda and powder drinks mixed with sugar are YUKS!
— How often do I eat? What time of the day? Eating a big meal before going to bed is not as desirable as eating the same big meal at lunchtime.
— How much do I eat? Do I have second helpings frequently? Do I eat more than my friends?
— Why do I eat when I am not hungry? When I am upset? When I am watching T. V.? When I am bored?
— How much do I exercise and what kind of exercise do I participate in? Any exercise is better than no exercise,

but there are activities such as jogging, fast walking, or biking that can be more beneficial towards fat loss than others. All of these activities use large muscles of the body, and therefore, burn a lot of calories. These activities can also speed up your metabolism. However, two important things must also be remembered when exercising. How long and how hard!

Think about...

— What kinds of foods you eat. Foods that are fried are high in fat or sugar and are not as good for you as foods that are not. A snack of popcorn without the butter is better than potato chips.

— Making a food diary for three to five days. Write down what you ate, what time you ate, what you were doing while you were eating (watching T.V., talking on the phone, etc.).

— What type of exercise you do.

Aerobic exercise, activities that keep your arms and legs moving for at least twenty minutes, burn more calories than other types of activities. Aerobic exercises can also speed up your metabolism. But you must do the exercise hard enough to challenge our body. Your breathing gets faster, your heart pumps faster, the exercise feels fairly hard, and your body is perspiring. Make your body work hard, but don't push yourself so hard that you are huffing and puffing and ready to drop! Examples of good aerobic exercises are jogging, fast walking, and biking.

Parents and students take note: Jan mentioned that one of her biggest pet peeves is when adults use food as a reward system. Food is for nutrition. Please don't be tempted to use such items as candy or cookies when your son or daughter achieves a goal. Positive reinforcement and praise are welcomed!

Girls, here's a really easy, nutritional recipe for you to try that Jan Johnson sends us. (She demonstrated this when the crew of "Good Morning, America" visited Super Club Kid's Fitness Club.)

Superkids Lasagna

1 jar all natural spaghetti sauce (no sugar, no meat)
Low-fat mozzarella cheese
Low-fat ricotta cheese
Uncooked lasagna noodles

Layer ingredients in a microwave-safe pan that will enable you to lay out the noodles flat. Finish layering with some of the mozzarella. Make sure noodles are totally covered with sauce. Microwave on medium level for thirty to thirty-five minutes. Bon Appetit!

Visit Super Club Kid's Fitness Clubs when they come to your town, or take part in a regular fitness program at your school or with your family.

Pretty Foods Vs. Ugly Foods

Pretty Foods	Ugly Foods
Big, crunchy apples	Potato chips
Grapes	Candy bars
Raisins	Cookies
Yogurt and wheat germ	Hot fudge sundae
Baked potato with a squeeze	French fries and ketsup
of lemon	3 or more pieces of pizza
1 or 2 pieces of pizza	Soda
Juice	
———————————	———————————
———————————	———————————
———————————	———————————

I'll bet you already have this one figured out. Right? Pretty foods are the ones you really like and ugly foods are the ones your folks force you to eat. Wrong! Pretty foods are the ones you *should* be eating, and of course, ugly foods are the ones you should avoid. Now, we didn't say *never* eat ugly foods. Do you think life would be fair if you were never allowed to eat birthday cake and ice cream? Of course not! But you're too smart to eat these things every day.

Can you add some pretty foods and ugly foods to our list?

"I Am What I Eat"
Quiz Scrambles

1. I am found in butter, meat, poultry, and dairy products. I keep you warm and give you energy.
   T S F A   = _____

2. You need me to keep your teeth and gums healthy. I keep your hair shiny and I even help your sweet disposition. You'll find me in fruits and vegetables, whole grain cereal, dairy products, and (yum) liver.
   I V I S N T M A   = _____

3. I build strong muscles and healthy tissue. You can find me in red meats, dried beans, milk, cheese, cereals, and eggs.
   O E P T R N I   = _____

4. I keep your bones sturdy, your blood rich and healthy, and your teeth strong. You can find me when you eat liver, milk products, cheese, vegetables, and drinking water treated with fluoride.
   E S L N A M R I   = _____

5. I give you the energy you need to be the prettiest you ever! I'm found in bread, cereal, fruits, vegetables, and (careful!) sweets.
   O Y S T C E A A R R D H B   = _____

Answers: (No Peeking!)

1. Fats   2. Vitamins

3. Protein   4. Minerals

5. Carbohydrates

131

A Guide to
Vitamins and Minerals

Vitamin	Will help my body to:	I will need to eat:
A	—Have healthy skin —Have good eyesight —Have strong bones and teeth	Liver, egg yolks, leafy green vegetables, whole milk, cheese, butter, sweet potatoes, apricots
D	—Use calcium and phosphorus to build strong bones and teeth	Whole milk, oily fish, egg yolk, and a moderate amount of sunlight on skin
E	—Use vitamins A and C better —Prevent cell damage	Wheat germ oil, vegetable oils, green vegetables, nuts, margarine
K	—Keep blood healthy; aids in normal clotting	Liver, egg yolks, kale, lettuce, spinach, cabbage
C	—Hold body cells together —Heal wounds and broken bones —Resist infection —Keep gums and teeth healthy	Citrus fruits and juices, strawberries, canteloupe, tomatoes, broccoli, green vegetables, potatoes
Thiamin (B1)	—Turn carbohydrates into energy —Keep nervous system healthy	Whole grain breads and cereals, pork, liver, poultry, fish, peanuts
Riboflavin (B2)	—Use proteins, fats, and carbohydrates to produce energy to build tissue —Maintain healthy facial skin and eyes	Milk and milk products, meat, liver, eggs, green leafy vegetables, breads and cereals
Niacin (B3)	—Use carbohydrates for energy —Use oxygen to release energy —Keep nervous system healthy	Fish, poultry, meats, whole grain or enriched breads, nuts
Vitamin B6	—Use protein —Form red blood cells —Use body fat for energy	Pork, liver, cereal, poultry, fish, spinach
Vitamin B12	—Produce red blood cells —Keep nervous system healthy —Build new protein	Liver, kidney, meat, fish, milk, eggs
Folacin	—Produce red blood cells —Use carbohydrates, fats and protein	Liver, legumes, green leafy vegetables
Biotin	—Use proteins, fats and carbohydrates properly	Liver, egg yolks, dark green vegetables, kidney beans

132

A Guide to Good Eating

Use Daily

Milk Group

Three or more glasses milk—children
Smaller glasses for some children under nine
Four or more glasses—teen-agers
Two or more glasses—adults
Cheese, ice cream, and other milk-made foods can supply
part of the milk

Meat Group

Two or more servings
Meats, fish, poultry, eggs or cheese with dry beans, peas,
nuts as alternatives

Vegetables & Fruits

Four or more servings
Include dark green or yellow vegetables, citrus fruit, or tomatoes

Breads & Cereals

Four or more servings
Enriched or whole grain; added milk improves
nutritional values

How Much of You is Enough? Few things can be more upsetting than growing up "different." I'm not talking about different in the sense that your parents may be divorced or that your clothes may be different. I'm talking about being overweight. Being overweight robs you of your self-confidence and can also steal your energy.

The next time you're tempted to really stuff yourself on some of your favorite munchies or snacks, read this:

Snack	Calories
Small chocolate bar	300
1 piece pizza	185
1 eight ounce glass chocolate milk	200
Hot fudge sundae	430
1 slice apple pie	265
1 pancake (before the butter and syrup)	110

Calories add up very quickly. Some girls overeat when they are happy, some when they are sad, some...both!

Growing up as an overweight child can be a very traumatic experience. Habits are formed at an early age, and when you're young you really have no choice but to eat what is provided for you. However, you can make suggestions to your mom when she goes to the grocery store such as, "Gee, Mom. I really appreciate the cookies, but could you buy some pears and oranges the next time?"

If you are an overweight child, you will probably be an overweight teen, and you could possibly be an overweight adult. It is so much easier to lose weight when you are young. Now is the time to break all of the bad habits and form new healthy ones for your future.

The exercise routine that follows is basic and fun. It will take about one-half hour and should be done while you are listening to your favorite music. Why don't you take turns doing your exercise routine at a different friend's house each time and have your own little group session. The more the merrier, you know!

The Official Pretty Me Training Camp Routine

For safety and comfort, try these on a mat or thick beach towel.

1. *Reach for the Sky*—On tip toes, stretch *way* up; then, flop down like a rag doll. Do ten for warm-up.

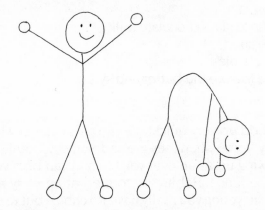

2. *Jumpin' Jack Flash*—Hands up, clap and jump up, then jump down; repeat twenty times. Really gets your blood going, great toner.

3. Whirly Bird—Ten small circles (with straight arms) forward, ten back, then ten large forward and ten back. This is great for wriggly arms.

4. Push-Aways—Stand slightly more than arm's length away from wall. Fingertips sould be touching wall. Do push-ups as if you were on the ground. Twenty, please. Great for arms and tummy.

5. *Pendulum*—Holding onto barre or chair back, swing leg forward and back, keeping toes pointed. Twenty each leg, please. Great for legs and firm bottoms!

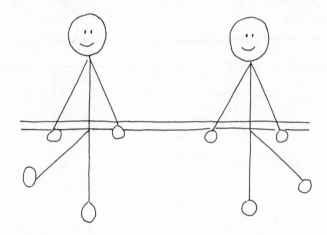

6. *Yo-yo*—"Stand" on knees, keep back straight; lean from side to side, touching knuckles to floor. Do twenty on each side; good for waists.

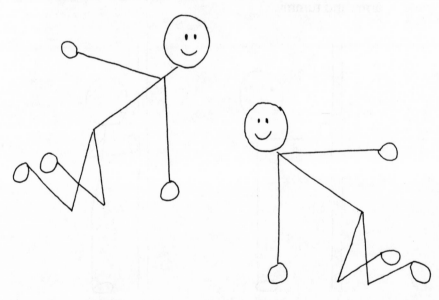

7. *Fancy Kicks*—Lay on side; raise leg up, then down, keeping toes pointed. Keeps upper thighs firm and upper hip area slim. Fifteen on each side.

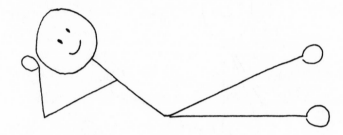

8. *Leg Lifts*—Lay very still while on floor. Now raise legs s-l-o-w-l-y while playing soothing music. Up and down ten times; for flat tummies.

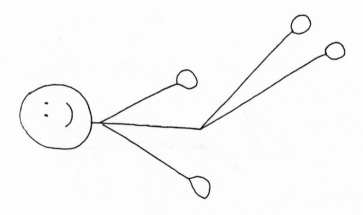

9. *Bottom Bounces*—Sit on floor and lean back on hands; now "walk" forward and backward (fifteen each way) on bottom. Gets rid of the jiggly-wigglies.

10. *Bumper Stumpers*—In same position as number nine, bounce back and forth on hips; first left, then right, etc. Ten on each side for slim hips.

Oh, go ahead—share this routine with your mom or older sister. You don't have to keep *all* the secrets to yourself.

Safety

Remember in our jigsaw puzzle that we stressed how important it is to be the best you can be and to always feel good about yourself? There are many parts of being your best that deal with outward appearance, but certainly by now, you know that what kind of "wrapper" a person comes in doesn't determine what kind of person they are on the inside.

Having a good head on your shoulders is just as important—and hopefully, that pretty head of yours is going to carry you through life as a happy, well-adjusted, very smart young lady.

We are going to discuss several types of safety rules because you are a busy girl, and you come in contact with lots of people as well as lots of different situations.

Let's start close to home.

Your Bedroom and Bathroom

Circle your response.

1. Are plastic bags destroyed or kept out of reach?	Yes	No
2. Is there a light within reach of your bed?	Yes	No
3. Does your bedroom have proper ventilation? (Does fresh air circulate?)	Yes	No
4. Are all room heaters turned off at bedtime?	Yes	No
5. Do you have a non-skid mat in your bath tub?	Yes	No
6. Are all medicines kept in locked cabinets away from children?	Yes	No
7. Are infants and toddlers watched while bathing?	Yes	No
8. Are all electrical appliances kept away from water and unplugged after use?	Yes	No
9. Does Mother throw all out-dated prescriptions away?	Yes	No

10. Do your curtains hang far away from
     sources of heat?   Yes   No

If you answered all ten questions "Yes," you're not just
pretty—you're smart!

Fire Safety

Circle your answer.

1. Fireplaces have screens or glass doors in
    front to stop sparks.   Yes   No
2. All heaters are kept away from curtains,
    furniture, clothing and papers.   Yes   No
3. Cords and wires do not hang where little
    children can pull them down.   Yes   No
4. Wires on lamps, radios, T.V.s, toasters, and
    hair dryers are not broken. (Ask an adult
    to check, please.)   Yes   No
5. Extension cords under carpets
    are removed.   Yes   No
6. Matches are kept out of reach
    of children.   Yes   No
7. People smoking cigarettes put them out
    carefully and completely in ashtrays.   Yes   No
8. My family knows that we should crawl very
    low in case of smoke in our house.   Yes   No
9. Our family has an escape plan. We know
    two ways out of our house and have
    decided on a meeting place outside.   Yes   No
10. The smoke detectors in our house work.
    We know because we check them
    every month.   Yes   No
11. The fire department telephone number is
    on our telephone.   Yes   No
12. Trash and old rags have been cleaned up
    and thrown away.   Yes   No

13. In case of fire, my family knows to STOP,
    DROP, and ROLL.   Yes   No
14. I know my complete house address   Yes   No
15. I know that I am never to play near fire
    or smoke.   Yes   No

If you answered numbers one to fifteen "Yes," thank you for helping to make your house a safer place.

Water Safety

Circle your answer

1. I know how to swim.   Yes   No
2. I never swim alone; I always use the
   buddy system.   Yes   No
3. If I'm on a boat, I always wear a bright
   orange life jacket.   Yes   No
4. I always stay seated when I'm in a
   small boat.   Yes   No
5. If I'm in a boat and it turns over I will hold
   on until help arrives.   Yes   No

All five "Yes" answers? Good job!

The One Time It's Okay to Say, "No, Thank You"

1. If drugs are ever offered to you, say "No!" and then quickly walk away.
2. If beer or other alcoholic beverages are offered, say "No!"
3. Don't hang around with anyone who uses drugs or alcohol *or* smokes cigarettes.
4. Don't go into areas where you know people use drugs or alcohol.
5. If someone continues to approach you, or if you know someone with a problem, ask your parents for help. Or

you can talk to your clergyman, your school counselor, or a trusted adult friend.

Your life is precious. Treasure yourself and keep your body and mind healthy for all the exciting things happening as you grow up.

Bicycle Safety. Most of you probably ride a bicycle from time to time. Perhaps you ride to school. You may just ride for fun after school, or some of you may be riding your bike as an athletic activity.

In some countries, bicycling is a main method of transportation. You can just imagine how careful you would have to be while riding your bike in a place like China with cars and pedestrians rushing all around at the same time!

Although bike riding is fun and enjoyable, it's not just a play-time activity; and a bicycle is not a *toy*! From the first moment you board your bicycle, you are the driver of a vehicle.

As a driver you are responsible for your own safety and for others on the road. You need to be familiar with dangers that you may face and the rules for safe cycling.

Over one thousand people are killed each year in the United States from bicycle collisions with automobiles. Most of them are children!

In addition to that horrible number you can add fifty thousand disabling injuries and five-hundred thousand minor injuries *each year*!

One of the first things to remember is to ride a bike that is right for your size. You will not be able to properly keep control of a bike that is too large or too small. If you or your folks are not sure exactly which size is right, go to a bicycle shop and be properly measured and "matched up" to a bike. You'll feel much more confident as you ride.

Here are some numbers to share with your parents or other adults:

— Most bicycle injuries and deaths involve children from five to fourteen years old.

— The most severe injuries occur at intersections.

— Seventy-five percent of all bicycling accidents happen during the spring and summer.
— Most youth bicycle accidents occur on Saturdays.
— Ninety percent of all reported bicycle accidents occur in residential areas.
— Ninety percent of all reported bicycle accidents occur in daylight.
— Seventy-five percent of all deaths of youths on bicycles occured from a blow to the head! PLEASE, wear a helmet (in your favorite color, of course)—your newest fashion accessory.

Girls, please read these safety tips, and pass them along to a friend.

Safe and Sound

— Please check your state and local regulations so that you'll know what kind of reflectors or additional safety features you must have.
— You must have a bell or a horn.
— Use a basket or a rack to carry books and other packages so that both hands will be free to control the bike.
— Do not carry friends on your bike unless it is equipped for them.
— Watch for parked cars pulling out in traffic and pedestrians stepping into your path.
— Check your tires, brakes, chains, and other parts frequently.
— Don't stunt or show off when you ride.
— Keep to the right and drive with traffic, never against it.
— Observe all traffic regulations as set up for cyclists in your community.
— Always remember your left hand signals. Glance over your shoulder before signaling, and when the traffic is heavy, get off your bike and *walk it.*
— Right turn—arm bent up at a ninety degree angle from your elbow.
— Left turn—arm held straight out from your shoulder.
— Slowing or Stopping—arm bent down from your elbow.

Riding your bicycle should be fun, useful, physically beneficial—and always SAFE!

Chapter V
Special Places

As you get older, you will be allowed to do more and more away from your home. You'll go to lots of special places and have opportunities to do many wonderful things. Whenever we are faced with new situations, there are possibilities of becoming nervous, feeling silly and getting embarrassed. These things can really take away from having a good time—and that's just not fair is it?

Let's discuss some of these different situations.

Being a House Guest

What a treat! You've been invited to spend the night with a classmate or perhaps an entire weekend with an out-of-town friend.

1. Be sure that both parents or other adult in charge say it's okay. Quite often, girls make overnight plans during school on Friday, only to discover that families have made other plans. That can really be disappointing.

2. Don't pack everything you own. Don't give Jill's mom the idea that you've moved in for good! For overnight neighborhood type sleep-overs, one tote bag with the basics is all you will need: toothbrush, pajamas, change of play clothes, and anything else special you need for additional activities. If you're going somewhere with your friend's entire family, make sure you know how much money you need to take with you, and be certain to let your family know exactly where you'll be.

3. For longer visits, you'll need an ample supply of clothing (underwear too), shampoo, conditioner, and any other personal items you may need so that you won't have to borrow things unless it's absolutely necessary.

4. Don't criticize the way your friend's family does things. Don't complain and say things like, "My mom doesn't make me do that." For a short time, you can adjust to things done a different way.

5. Offer to help around the house. Don't scatter your belongings all over, and don't act as though you're there to be waited on.

6. What a great opportunity to try out some new foods! Don't say, "Yuck, my mom never makes us eat that!" Say, "No, thank you," or better yet, try a little!

7. For sleep-overs at a classmate's house in your neighborhood, a short thank-you note should be written the first time you spend the night. After that, a sincere "Thank you, Mrs. Wilder. I had a wonderful time," is adequate.

8. For weekend visits (or longer), a lovely thank-you letter mailed *as soon* as you are home, as well as a small token gift is in order. Perhaps some potpourri or some scented soaps. The gift should be purchased ahead of time, wrapped and brought with you so that you may leave it before you depart.

9. Last, but absolutely not least—DON'T SNOOP!

Movies, Concerts, Theatre, Ballet

Movies. Please don't cut in line while waiting to enter. If you're waiting to purchase tickets and you spot Kerri ten people ahead of you, do not attempt to sweet talk her into letting you cut in line.

— Most movie theatres do not have ushers, but if you attend one that does, you'll walk slightly behind him or her. Ushers know the way and are usually carrying small flashlights.

— Refreshments are part of the fun of going to the movies, but you are responsible for discarding your trash.

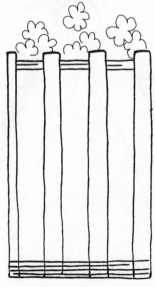

— When you are being seated or need to be excused, please say "Excuse me" as you pass in front of the other patrons. Do this with your back to the screen and facing the people you are saying "Excuse me" to.

— If you *must* say somthing to a friend during the movie, keep it to a whisper—and please keep it short.

— Silly noises and general "cutting up" do not belong in a movie theatre or in the other special places we're discussing.

Concerts, Theatre and Ballet. Do the very mention of these three activities cause your heart to race, your hands to perspire (ladies *never* sweat) and tempt you to stay home with a good book? (Like this one.) If so, you may be like lots of other kids who are simply a little frightened and intimidated to try something different.

Most schools are very good about offering field trips to such places and you can discuss what to expect before you attend as a class.

Concerts or recitals are when musicians perform live music.

Theatre is when actors perform on a stage in the same room that you're in.

Ballet is when dancers perform with graceful, wonderful movement. It's like theatre but with dancing instead of delivering lines.

The proper attire for such events is similar to what you would wear to church or to a wedding.

Please do not arrive late for such entertainment—early is better—maybe ten minutes or so to be certain you can find your seat. If you will be purchasing tickets at the box office, allow even more time.

If you are late, you will need to wait until there is a pause in the program to be seated.

If there is an usher, ladies follow him, and any gentlemen in the party follow the ladies.

Intermission is the time you may leave your seat for anything other than an emergency. It is usually from ten to twenty minutes. You may get a beverage at this time, go to the restroom, or critique the performance with friends and family.

Babysitting Guidelines

Some of you may be getting old enough to embark upon what is probably the first career for most of us—babysitting.

There may be some of you who get plenty of babysitting experience right in your own home with younger brothers and sisters! However, for the girls (and boys!) who enjoy young children, it is a great way to earn extra spending money.

Take it from a mom—good babysitters are a treasure to behold and become a very special part of a young child's life. Babysitting is a huge commitment and shouldn't be taken lightly.

Alma, a very special babysitter in our neighborhood, was quite a little businesswoman when she first moved in. She designed and printed a flyer introducing herself and noting her qualifications and interests, then took them door-to-door. Several days later she followed up with a cheerful visit to make sure we had received the flyer and to see if we had any questions.

Wow! My husband and I looked at each other and said, "I think we've got to give this kid a try!" We're glad we did. Alma even brings her own "goodie bag" of books and activities which she has collected so that her small charges have new and exciting things to do when she visits.

If you are trying to establish yourself as a good baby-sitter in your neighborhood, I strongly suggest this method of letting folks know you're ready for work.

But, before you do, let's make sure you understand just what a responsibility you're taking on.

1. It's not a bad idea to have your parents meet the parents of the child you are sitting for. It just helps everyone to feel a little more secure and that's what babysitting is all about.
2. Payment should be discussed before you accept the job. Different parts of the country pay different amounts, and there's no reason to put anyone in an embarrassing or uncomfortable situation after you've accepted the assignment.
3. Make sure that the child's parents show you where everything is in the house that you may need—telephone book, fire extinguisher, band-aids, extra blankets, etc.
4. Be certain that you have any and all phone numbers where you can reach the parents or other responsible adults in case of an emergency (perhaps a neighbor's number as a back-up). Don't call for silly things; it will alarm the parents.
5. If one or both of the parents use a pager or "beeper," make sure that you know how to make contact properly.
6. If the child is on medication, ask if you are supposed to give it to him/her, and if so, find out what time and *exactly* what amount.

7. Ask if there is a neighbor you should go to in case of an emergency. Also, have the police, fire, and rescue phone numbers close by. Make a point of knowing the house number and street of the home you are in.

8. Find out exactly what you're supposed to do. Do you feed the child? What time does he or she go to bed? Are snacks allowed? Are you supposed to give the child a bath?

9. Do not spank children that you are babysitting for. Saying "No" or giving time-outs for unacceptable behavior is usually alright. What often works well is to find a new game or activity for them to do.

10. Do *not* bring friends with you or have anyone visit while you're working unless you have received permission from the parents.

11. *Please* do not tie up the telephone! Nothing upsets parents more than trying time after time to get through to *their* house to check on *their* child.

12. Find out which beverages or snacks you are allowed to have. I heard of one very embarrassing situation where a sitter sampled a cake that a mom made for a special occasion! Shame on them both for not asking, or explaining.

13. Please try to stay awake until the parents return unless they're going to be very late and allow you to lie down near the child's room and a telephone.

14. Ask if the child is allowed to watch television. Are any programs off limits? If you watch TV after the child is asleep, please keep the volume down so that you can hear any sounds coming from his or her room.

15. Last, but certainly not least, say "Thank you" to the parents when they pay you.

Good babysitting skills are well remembered and can add up to some very nice benefits for you.

Many schools, scouting groups, and the Red Cross offer babysitting classes from time to time. It's well worth your effort. Basic child care and first aid skills are covered.

Have fun and get a BIG piggy bank!

School Courtesy

Between school, eating, sleeping, sports, and music, I'll bet you don't have lots of extra time. After all, you do need to sleep for about eight hours each evening. School probably takes about that long and that leaves you only eight hours for everything else!

Remember the beauty routine we did earlier? Now you see why it's so helpful. School takes up about one-third of your life. When you finish school and have a career, it will take up at least that much time.

What point am I trying to make? It sure would be nice if you liked what you were doing during those eight hours.

There's no reason for you to dread going to school each day. I was one of those kids who basically enjoyed school. There's no real secret to make you like school. It's your *attitude* that makes the difference. If you go somewhere and have yourself convinced that you'll have a horrible time, you'll be correct—you'll have a horrible time. Being cheerful is contagious to your friends and teachers. Be careful—you may catch it!

School should be an adventure each day. Every day can be new and exciting—like a special journey. If you will leave your house each morning with a happy, cooperative disposition, you will definitely be the winner.

Do you have a "clown" or trouble-maker in any of your classes? Did you laugh the first few times they acted up, but then it began to seem silly and babyish? Sure you did. It's wise not to encourage someone who is goofing around because in some ways it makes you just as guilty as they are, and of course, it only encourages them.

Locker Etiquette. As you get older, you'll be assigned a locker in the hallway at school where you will store coats, school books, lunch, and all sorts of goodies. Chances are you will share this locker with another student who you may or may not already know. Can you imagine sharing a bedroom with a stranger? It may take a little extra patience in the beginning, but with all of your new friendship skills and charm, you'll probably make a new friend!

Beleive me, there's nothing more hectic than those few precious moments between classes when you rush to your locker to unload or reload materials. Be courteous to the neighbors on either side of you, and don't crowd the person you share with. Neatness counts here just as importantly as in your bedroom!

Getting Attention-For All The Right Reasons. When was the last time the teacher asked a question and somebody practically came out of their seat trying to gain his or her attention? Acting silly or making loud noises to gain attention or approval turns most teachers off. Raising your hand quietly and confidently will impress your teachers much more.

Am I Keeping You Awake? You're probably not as familiar with how a classroom looks from the teacher's view as you are from your desk, but take it from one who knows, it can be a pretty lonely place to stand.

When you hold your head up with your hands, slump into your chair, and stare around the classroom, you give the impression that you'd rather be somewhere else. Wouldn't you feel just awful if you were teaching your class a wonderful new piece of knowledge (or at least you thought you were) and they all looked half asleep? Sure you would.

Please give your teachers the respect they deserve. Your enthusiasm and interest will wear off on them and vice-versa.

Field Trips. The very sound of the words excite most of you. You're going someplace special with your class. You'll probably ride on a bus, and it will be a different routine for your day.

Let's remember a few basic rules to assure everyone of a good time:

— Always stay with the group. Don't be tempted to wander.
— Wear name tags if they are provided.
— If you're riding a bus, stay seated and wear seatbelts at all times.
— Be certain that you have an ample amount of spending money so you won't encounter embarrassing situations.
— If parents or other students are acting as chaperones or

helpers, please give them the same respect you would your teachers.

The New Kid on the Block. What can be the most exciting *and* the most horrible feeling all at the same time? Right! Being the "new girl."

Everyone is staring at you. "What is she wearing?" "Where does she live?" "Look at the way she wears her hair!" It can make even the most confident girl have jiggly knees!

However, starting a new school in a new town can be so much fun. It's a brand new opportunity to be your very best. Try to stay calm on your first day. Wear a special outfit that always makes you feel your best. The only other accessories you'll need will be a sincere smile and a cheery personality!

Still, there may be times when you're really down-in-the-dumps and miss your old friends dreadfully. Ask your parents if a short, long-distance telephone call can be arranged—or sit down and write an upbeat letter about your exciting moving experience.

If your parents are in the military or work for the government, you may already be used to the adjustment that must be made when you move. Look at the bright side— you'll have lots of wonderful friends all over the world!

Church Courtesy

Many families attend some sort of church or synagogue service at least once a week. Attending church helps you to become a better person. Religion can help you to understand your family and friends better—and yourself.

If I spent the night with a friend on Saturday night, I was allowed to attend her church on Sunday. I have always been fascinated with what others did, and occasionally going to church with my Catholic friend was very interesting—just as she enjoyed attending our Presbyterian church. Many of your friends probably attend different churches. Always be on your best behavior when attending any church or temple.

You will want to wear neat, clean clothes—nothing trendy or "loud." Please be on time. If you are running late, please wait until an usher shows you to a seat.

Once I was a little older, I was allowed to sit with friends from my Sunday school class during the church service instead of sitting with my family. That decision is up to your parents, but if you do sit with a friend, it doesn't give you permission to talk, look at books, doodle, or otherwise pass the time with other projects. Even if you don't fully understand the service, please save any comments, questions, or criticism until after you have left the church.

If you are nervous about knowing what to do in an unfamiliar church, observe carefully and do what the other people do as far as sitting, standing, kneeling, etc. You show a special kind of respect and friendship when you practice good manners while attending a friend's church as well as your own.

Conclusion

This book has come to an end, but your exciting journey through youth is in its prime!

Keep this book handy so that you can refer to it whenever you're going someplace special or facing a new experience. Take good care of your *Pretty Me* book, and one day, perhaps, your own daughter will enjoy it!

In the mean time, just remember this:

...and I'm the very best ME that I can be!

About the Author

Linda G. Wilder Dyer is president of Pretty Me, Inc., a company specializing in self-improvement books and courses for girls of all ages. She is the author of a companion volume, *Finishing Touches For Teens* (1991), and has taught charm and modeling courses for all ages for over nineteen years, but especially enjoys teaching girls who are striving for self-confidence and a positive self-image.

She is married, lives in Virginia Beach, Virginia, and has two daughters, Ashley and Elizabeth, with whom she shares her extensive bear and doll collection.